Clippings from My Notebook

CORRIE TEN BOOM, subject of the best-selling book and popular film *The Hiding Place*, was born in Amsterdam in 1892, and a short while later the family moved to Haarlem where she grew up. *The Hiding Place* chronicled her experiences in protecting Jews from the Nazis during World War II and her own subsequent imprisonment. Since the war she has been a prolific author and speaker of world-wide reputation, and has received several awards and honours. A severe stroke in 1978 forced her to remain housebound in her home in California, from where she continues her ministry by sharing with you these 'clippings from her notebook'.

Clippings from My Notebook

WRITINGS AND SAYINGS COLLECTED BY

Corrie ten Boom

First published in the USA 1982
First published in Great Britain 1983
Triangle
SPCK
Holy Trinity Church
Marylebone Road
London NW1 4DU

British Library Cataloguing in Publication Data

ten Boom, Corrie
  Clippings from my notebook.
  1. Christian life
  I. Title
  248.4   BV4501.2
  ISBN 0-281-04034-6

  Filmset, printed and bound in Great Britain by
  Hazell Watson & Viney Ltd, Aylesbury, Bucks

Contents

Foreword

Corrie ten Boom, the youngest of four children, was born on April 15, 1892, in Amsterdam, The Netherlands. Her father, Casper ten Boom, was a watchmaker, and when Corrie was still a baby, the family moved to Haarlem where he inherited the family watchshop. Her godly and loving parents reflected the love of the heavenly Father, and when Corrie was five years old she accepted Jesus Christ as her Saviour and Lord. She witnessed for Him and prayed for the conversion of those in her neighbourhood all through her childhood years.

The ten Boom family home above the watchshop at Barteljorisstraat 19 (called Beje, pronounced 'bay-yay,' for short) had wide open doors to everybody and especially to those who were in need. Apart from Mr. and Mrs. ten Boom and the four children, the little home was shared by three aunts and later by a succession of foster children.

Corrie became the first woman to be a licensed watchmaker in The Netherlands, but she always said that she never became an expert at it because she was constantly busy with the carrying out of many plans. There were, for example, the clubs she ran – for boys and girls and for mentally retarded children and adults – and a Christian girl guide movement which in due course comprised thousands of members throughout The Netherlands, Indonesia, and the Dutch Antilles.

In 1844 an unusual event for that time took place. Casper ten Boom's grandfather started a prayer meeting in the Beje for the Jewish people. The ten Boom family loved the Jews, and when Casper ten Boom became involved in hiding and rescuing some of them during the Second World War, he replied, on being warned of the danger involved, 'If I die in prison, it will be an honour to have given my life for God's ancient people.' He did give his life for them. He and all his children were betrayed and arrested. He died, aged eighty-four, after ten days of imprisonment. Corrie and Betsie, her sister, were transported to Ravensbrück concentration camp where, after many privations in 'the deepest hell that man can create' but with a radiant testimony to the love of God, Betsie died in December 1944. Corrie was released a short time afterwards through a clerical error.

After her release, Corrie dedicated her life to telling others what she and Betsie had learned in Ravensbrück: 'There is no pit so deep that the love of Jesus Christ is not deeper still.' Corrie brought this message to sixty-four countries during thirty-three years of travel. An important part of her message was that when God tells us to forgive our enemies, He gives us the strength and love with which to obey.

I first met Tante Corrie ('aunt' in Dutch) when she was in her seventies, and one of the things that greatly impressed me was her desire to get to know and serve the Lord Jesus better. She was willing to learn from old and young, rich and poor, intellectual and uneducated. Once while attending a funeral with her I saw her making copious notes of the message which a young minister was giving. Later I became her co-worker and travelled with her for a while. Her notebook was always handy. When in 1977 she made her home in California, one of the first things she did was to send for the large pile of notebooks which, one by one, had accompanied her through the years. How she enjoyed going through them. Through her magazine, *The Hiding Place*, she passed on to her prayer partners 'clippings from her notebook'. We now pass these on to you.

In 1978, Tante Corrie's very active life of speaking, writing, and making films was cut off overnight by a serious stroke which took her speaking, reading, and writing abilities. Successive strokes partially paralysed her, and now, at nearly ninety years of age, she is confined to bed, in an extremely weak state; but still she radiates the love, peace, and victory of the Lord Jesus. Her joyful countenance greatly challenges and blesses all who see it. It is her prayer as she shares with you these sayings, writings, and favourite Scripture verses that He will be glorified.

PAMELA ROSEWELL
Co-worker of Corrie ten Boom

Good News

> 'How beautiful are the feet of them that preach the gospel of peace, and bring glad tidings of good things!'
> Romans 10.15 KJV

There are so many people living close to all of us who do not know the Lord Jesus and who need to have His great love explained to them. If we do not do it, who will? The time is short, eternity is so very long. Let us be busy in the Lord's work and ask Him to use us to bring others to Him.

Once in Switzerland a mother brought me her little daughter who was ten years old. She said, 'Can you tell this girl how to become a child of God? She always goes to Sunday school, and really knows everything, but I can't tell her what to do to become a child of God.'

I took the girl aside and said, 'Look, imagine that I wanted to adopt you as my child. Once I had the proper papers I could just say, "Now you are my child". But I wouldn't do it that way. I would wait until I saw that you liked me and then I would ask you, "Do you want to become my child?"

'Then, if you should say, "Yes, I would like to become your child very much", I would continue and tell you, "All right, here are the papers. They have been ready for a long time. I did not use them until now because you had not decided that you loved me and wanted to become my child."

'The Lord Jesus asks you now, "Will you become a child of God?" If you say, "Yes, Lord, I will," He will tell you, "All is ready. The preparations were all taken care of at the cross. I have paid the price so that you can become a child of God. We have waited for the decision to come from you." '

Then I read with her John 1.12: 'As many as received him, to them gave he power to become the sons of God, even to them that believe on his name' (KJV).

We knelt down after that and the girl accepted the Lord. I can tell you her happy face was more beautiful than the snow-capped Alps on the horizon. Is it really so simple?

In Germany a woman told me that forty-two years ago she had committed a terrible sin and since then she had prayed every day for forgiveness. Poor soul! She did not know, like so many people do not know, that the sin problem has been solved at Calvary's cross.

The moment that you believe, you are registered in heaven as one of those who has rights and privileges that make you a multi-millionaire in the spiritual realm. Faith is a problem for those who do not know the Bible and the Lord. God says, ' . . . I am watching over my word to perform it' (Jeremiah 1.12 RSV). When the heart has learned to trust Him as He should be trusted – utterly, without reservation – then the Lord throws wide the doors of the treasure-house of grace. He bids us to come in with boldness so that we may receive our share of the inheritance of the saints in life.

The Bible is full of overflowing riches and victory.

2

'The Father . . . who hath blessed us with all spiritual blessings . . . in Christ' (Ephesians 1.3 KJV) means that the moment we accept Jesus Christ as our Saviour and confess Him as our Lord, everything God wrought in Christ belongs to us. It is ours. Often people say, 'I hope that I am a child of God,' or, 'I try to be a Christian.' I believe that we are too often failure-conscious. Faith makes us victory-conscious. Faith brings the unreality of hope to the reality of now. Hope is future. Faith is present. Faith is the radar that shows us the reality of Christ's victory. The moment that radar works correctly, we dare to say, 'God has made me able to conquer weakness, fear, and inability, and I stand and declare that whosoever believes in Jesus shall not be put to shame.'

Jesus was Victor, Jesus is Victor, Jesus will be Victor. Hallelujah!

Security is having the Word of God in your own language. Peace is having the Word of God in your own heart.

Add all the love of all the parents in the whole world and the total sum cannot be multiplied enough times to express God's love for me, the least of His children (see Ephesians 3.14–19).

A Child Shall Lead Them

'. . . whoever does not receive the kingdom of God like a child shall not enter it.'

Luke 18.17 RSV

Children can be such joyful additions to our so often serious and stuffy world. They open our eyes to the wonders of creation and make us consider such important questions as, 'How do the stars stay in the sky?' and 'Why is the grass green instead of red?' Their laughter brightens many lives.

In my years of travelling I was often touched by children because of their honesty and open expressions of emotion. They aren't afraid to admit weakness, yet they will often defend what they know to be right, regardless of the circumstances or possible results.

I remember one story of an East German teacher who told her class that God does not exist. After her lesson, she asked who still believed in God, and a little girl stood up. The teacher made her stay after school and write one hundred times, 'I do not believe God exists.' The girl could not do that, so she wrote, 'I do believe God exists.' The teacher was so angry with her that she made her write it correctly one thousand times at home that night. The little girl wrote it one thousand times her way, although she knew she would be punished severely in school the next day. This young child believed in God and was not going to deny Him in spite of the consequences. What an important lesson for all of us to learn!

In addition to being open about their feelings, children have a very special freedom in their communication with their heavenly Father. They aren't held back by the barriers that adults build between themselves and the Lord.

A mother I met told me that she saw her little boy sitting in a corner of the room, saying 'A-B-C-D-E-F-G. . . .'

'What are you doing?' she asked.

'Mom, you told me I should pray, but I have never prayed in my life and I don't know how. So I gave God the whole alphabet and asked Him to make a good prayer of it.'

That boy understood a little bit of what Paul wrote in Romans 8.26 – that the Holy Spirit Himself helps us to pray.

Another very important lesson we can learn from children is seen in their relationship with their parents. In my family we knew that we were loved. Our parents had our very best interests in mind; there was never any doubt about that. They were totally trustworthy, and in our home we children always felt secure and protected. Our parents' love for us was an excellent introduction to the relationship we came to share with our heavenly Father. We are His precious children. His love for us is so great that we can't even begin to understand it. In the midst of hurrying about and being concerned with so many details of daily living, we must always remember that God's love can make us conquerors if we receive Him as a child – with an open and trusting heart.

The Three Locks

> '*Let us search and try our ways, and turn again to the* Lord.'
>
> Lamentations 3.40 KJV

Three times in my life locks were closed behind me and, after a time of imprisonment, opened again.

I learned how it feels to be behind a door that can be opened only from the outside. Those were difficult classes in life's school, but in a difficult class one learns much, especially when there is a good teacher.

My Teacher was the Lord. He made me learn from experience that, for a child of God, a pit can be very deep, but always below us are the everlasting arms of our Lord.

The first lock that closed behind me left me in a cell where I was in solitary confinement for about four months. In my book *Prison Letters* you can read what a miracle of blessing I experienced. The fellowship with the Lord was so precious that I wrote to friends outside, 'Please never worry about me; sometimes it may be dark, but the Saviour provides His light and how wonderful that is. I am surprised that I can adjust so well to being alone in a prison cell.'

My sister Betsie, who was in a different cell, wrote, 'This horror has come to us from God's loving hands to purify me.'

When the second lock closed behind Betsie and

me, we were in Vught concentration camp where I learned another lesson. I wrote from Vught, 'We are in God's training school and learning much. We are continually protected by the most extraordinary providence, and we know that we can hold out in spite of the hard life. God knows the way; we are at peace with everything.'

The third lock was closed behind us in Ravensbrück, the terrible concentration camp north of Berlin. For Betsie, the lock was opened when the Lord took her to Him.

> To enter into Heaven's rest
> And yet to serve the Master blest,
> From service good, to service
>   best.

For me the door opened to a wide, wide world where I became a tramp for the Lord, going wherever I could tell what I had learned: that when the worst happens in the life of a child of God, the best remains and the very best is yet to be.

I have seen many people behind closed doors in the more than sixty countries where I have worked. Some were behind the solid rock of hatred. Many were liberated through claiming Romans 5.5 and by asking forgiveness for their sins.

'Forgiveness is the key that unlocks the door of resentment and the handcuffs of hatred. It is a power that breaks the chains of bitterness and the shackles of selfishness.' Whom the Lord makes free, is free indeed – that I saw in the lives of people who were behind the locks of bondage to drugs, alcohol, and smoking.

Self is a tight lock. I saw many decent sinners who were in a kind of spiritual prison because self was on the throne of their hearts and Jesus was on the cross. What a liberation came when Jesus cleansed the heart with His blood. Then He came to the throne, and self went on the cross.

My friends, is there still a closed lock in your life? Jesus is willing to set you free.

Do not struggle to get out of rough hands. God uses rough hands to make us beautiful and perfect. Of Jesus we read: 'The soldiers plaited a crown of thorns, and put it on his head . . .' (John 19.2 KJV). 'I gave my back to the smiters and . . . I hid not my face from shame and spitting' (Isaiah 50.6 KJV). He had power to help Himself, but He never used it.

'Share in suffering as a good soldier of Christ Jesus. . . . An athlete is not crowned unless he competes according to the rules' (2 Timothy 2.3,5 RSV).

'God hath not given us the spirit of fear, but of power and of love and of a sound mind' (2 Timothy 1.7 KJV).

The Power of Prayer

'. . . come boldly unto the throne of grace, that [you] may obtain mercy, and find grace to help in time of need.'

Hebrews 4.16 KJV

When I was a little girl I was sure that Jesus was a member of the ten Boom family. It was just as easy to talk to Him as it was to carry on a conversation with my mother and father. Jesus was there. I was closer to the reality and truth of Jesus' presence than the one who makes fellowship with the Lord a problem by reasoning and logical thinking.

Prayer is a joy and a privilege, available to all of God's children. The Lord longs to hear all of our concerns – any concern too small to be turned into a prayer is too small to be made into a burden.

My father prayed because he had a good Friend with whom to share the problems of the day. He prayed because he had a direct connection with his Maker when he had a concern. He prayed because there was so much for which he was thankful.

Prayers should be informal and to the point – conversation with God, so to speak. Remember, prayer is not one-way traffic. If it were, it would be similar to someone coming into your house, asking a question, and then leaving without waiting for an answer. Prayer is both asking and receiving, speaking and listening. Yes, that takes time. But you can learn how to converse with God.

An important thing to remember when praying is that Jesus is our Advocate before the Father. When we begin or end our prayers with 'in the name of Jesus,' it is just as if Jesus Himself is saying, 'Father, this is a prayer from your beloved child, Mary [or John or Carol, . . .].' That prayer is sanctified by the name of Jesus. The name that is above every other in heaven or on earth is Jesus. Saviour! He is our strength. '. . . There is salvation in no one else, for there is no other name under heaven given among men by which we must be saved' (Acts 4.12 RSV).

Jesus' example of intercession is one we should follow. The greatest thing one person can do for another is to pray for him. If at this moment you pray for someone, even though he is on the other side of the globe, the Lord Jesus will touch him.

When I am fearful or anxious for myself, I pray for others. I pray for everyone who comes into my thoughts – people with whom I have travelled, those who were in prison with me, my school friends of years ago. My fear soon disappears. Interceding for others releases me.

However, prayer should never be an excuse for inaction. Nehemiah prayed, but he also set guards for protection. He used common sense. As a result, what had not been done in a hundred years was finished in fifty-two days.

Sometimes God's answers to our prayers are not as clear to us as was His response to Nehemiah. But we must never doubt that God hears our prayers. Often when we think that God has not answered, He is saying, 'Wait.' His timing is perfect.

In order to receive answers we need to pray specific

prayers. God does not give stones for bread. By asking for specific things, we will receive specific answers. Most of us do not receive because we do not ask (see James 4.2).

Prayer is powerful. The devil smiles when we make plans. He laughs when we get too busy. But he trembles when we pray – especially when we pray together. Remember, though, that it is God who answers, and He always answers in a way that He knows is best for everyone.

Away with work that hinders prayer,
'Twere best to lay it down.
For prayerless work, however good,
Will fail to win the crown.

When we pray we step inside the room of the general headquarters of God. We may enter through Jesus who is the Way. Our inability meets God's ability, and then miracles happen.

Expect resistance but pray for miracles.

When man listens, God speaks.
When man obeys, God acts.
When man prays, God empowers.

Eternity

A man may go to heaven
without health
without wealth
without fame
without a great nature
without learning
without big earning
without culture
without beauty
without friends
without ten thousand other things,
but he never can go to heaven
without Christ.

The measure of a life, after all, is not its duration but its donation.

This life is only the first page of the book, not the last page.

'My times are in thy hand . . .' (Psalm 31.15 KJV).

I Was in Prison, but He Was With Me

> 'Be strong and courageous! Do not tremble or be dismayed, for the LORD your God is with you wherever you go.'

> Joshua 1.9 NASB

Do you ever feel alone? What a question! Of course you do. But I know from my own experience that the worst loneliness is that of solitary confinement.

Years ago I was alone in a cell for four months. One day for the first time a beam of sunlight shone through the window. I jumped up and stood so that the sunshine touched my face. Slowly it moved on and I moved too, just to enjoy that beam as long as possible.

That was one of the moments when I realized my loneliness as never before. I cried to the Lord, and He answered: 'Have you forgotten that there is always, under all circumstances, the sunshine of My love? Have I not said: "Lo, I am with you alway, even unto the end of the world" [Matt. 28.20]? I am your peace. I can give you joy now also.'

I started to sing, first softly, later more loudly:

> *What a friend we have in Jesus,*
> *All our sins and griefs to bear.*
> *What a privilege to carry*
> *Everything to God in prayer.*

I waited a moment, and then I heard from another cell:

> *O what peace we often forfeit,*
> *O what needless pain we bear,*
> *All because we do not carry*
> *Everything to God in prayer.*

It was an answer from a woman who also was in solitary confinement. Her husband had been shot before her eyes, then she had been put in prison. But she too knew Jesus as her Friend and Saviour. I answered her by singing:

> *Have we trials and temptations?*
> *Is there trouble anywhere?*
> *We should never be discouraged*
> *Take it to the Lord in prayer!*
>
> *Can we find a friend so faithful,*
> *Who will all our sorrows share?*
> *Jesus knows our every weakness,*
> *Take it to the Lord in prayer.*

A guard banged on the door and shouted: 'If you do not stop singing, I will take you to the dark cell.'

I stopped singing and threw myself onto my dirty bed. There was peace in my heart. The guard did not know when I sang so softly that only my Saviour could hear:

> *Are we weak and heavy-laden*
> *Cumbered with a load of care?*
> *Precious Saviour, still our refuge*
> *Take it to the Lord in prayer.*

14

> Do thy friends despise, forsake thee?
> Take it to the Lord in prayer!
> In His arms He'll take and shield thee,
> Thou wilt find a solace there.

Not only in solitary confinement can one feel alone. Often in the company of many others with whom you have no real fellowship you can be lonely. But Jesus is with you also. Have you asked Him to come into your heart? Then you can talk to Him without saying one word aloud. He hears and He loves you. You are very precious in His eyes. Hallelujah, what a Saviour!

I have held many things in my hands, and I have lost them all; but whatever I have placed in God's hands, that I still possess.

Someone said to me: 'When I worry I go to the mirror and say to myself: This tremendous thing which worries me is beyond solution; especially it is too hard for Jesus Christ to handle. After I have said so, I smile and am ashamed.'

I looked at Jesus and the dove of peace entered my heart! I looked at the dove of peace . . . and lo, off it went!

The Cure for Care*

> '. . . casting all your anxiety upon Him, because He cares for you.'
>
> 1 Peter 5.7 NASB

We imagine that a little anxiety and worry are indications of how wise we are. We think we see the dangers of life clearly. In reality, however, our fears are only an indication of how wicked we really are.

As Charles G. Trumbull says,

> Worry is sin; a black, murderous, God-defying, Christ-rejecting sin; worry about anything, at any time whatever. We will never know victory over worry and anxiety until we begin to treat it as sin. For such it is. It is a deep-seated distrust of the Father, who assures us again and again that even the falling sparrow is in His tender care.

The words *fear not* occur many times in the Bible. The Word of God has no suggestions, only commandments. So if we fear and worry, we are being disobedient, and disobedience is always a sin.

The only way blunders and destruction can occur in our lives is when we forget to trust God. When we take things into our own unskilled hands, we get them knotted and tangled.

Worry is utterly useless. It never serves a good purpose. It brings no good results. One cannot think or see clearly when worrying. Let pagans worry if they will, but we must not, for we have a living Saviour, our Lord Jesus Christ, and His conquering power. His victory can be our victory. Life at best is brief, and there is so much to be accomplished. If we must burn ourselves out, let us burn out for God.

In this age of increasing pace, it is easy to follow the crowd and let materialism become our god. But if we do, too often we find that worry and tension become our masters. The effects of tension are seen in all spheres of life. Tension leads to inefficiency and frayed nerves with our fellow workers and students; in politics, to strain in international relations and fears of war. In the home, tension leads to irritability with our husband or wife, destroying the very thing God meant to be perfect.

When we are worrying, we are not trusting. Yet we who have burdens and responsibilities are inclined to worry. Again, it is so important that we recognize the enemy. Worry and depression are sister and brother. I want to tell you about something that I experienced – a time when the influence of depression was practically nationwide.

After I was released from the German concentration camp, I returned to Holland until the war was over. Then God told me to go back to Germany, to carry the good news of Christ's victory over fear and guilt. When I arrived in Germany, however, I found the people in great confusion. Many German people had beloved relatives missing. Were they still in Russian concentration camps? Had they died in battle or in the horrible bombings? This uncertainty drove many people to desperation.

Many of these people were turning to the fortune-tellers to find their answers. While the evil spirits, working through the fortune-tellers, often gave just enough accurate information to keep the people coming back, something else also happened. Many of those who visited the fortune-tellers later developed horrible fears, depression, and anxiety. Their hearts, it seemed, were always in the gloom of darkness. They often had the urge to commit suicide. I immediately recognized this as a sure evidence of demon influence.

Jesus said, '. . . I am the Light of the world. So if you follow me, you won't be stumbling through the darkness, for living light will flood your path' (John 8.12 TLB). Even if a child of God has visited a fortune-teller and come under demon influence, he does not need to remain in darkness. He can be set free.

Realizing this, I began speaking against the sins of the occult. It was the occult that was putting people in bondage, causing them to break down mentally and spiritually. I often read Deuteronomy 18.10–13 to point out how these sins are an abomination in the sight of God. Instead of depending on God's power, the people were rushing to the enemy for help. And as we know, the enemy is a liar whose very purpose is to deceive people and lead them away from the truth.

I showed the German Christians how Jesus Christ has provided an answer to this serious problem. Satan is not the Victor, Jesus is. And even if the people had invited the demons in, Christ could overcome that. They did not have to live with their depression or fear any more. They had to be set free. I was able to say to them:

> . . . [God] gave you a share in the very life of Christ, for he forgave all your sins, and blotted out the charges proved against you, the list of his commandments which you had not obeyed. He took this list of sins and destroyed it by nailing it to his cross. In this way God took away Satan's power to accuse you of sin, and God openly displayed to the whole world Christ's triumph at the cross where your sins were all taken away (Colossians 2.13–15 TLB).

In the Old Testament there is an interesting story of the lost axehead. A 'son of the prophets' had been chopping wood and his axehead had fallen into the Jordan River. Since it was a borrowed axe, he was worried and afraid. He ran to Elisha for help. Elisha sent him back to the place where he had made his mistake, so the miracle of restoration could happen. The axehead floated to the surface, and the young man grabbed it and replaced it on the handle (see 2 Kings 6.1–7).

Just so, you need to go back to the place where you opened the door of your life to the influence of the spirit of worry. Where did the fear enter? What was it that caused you to start worrying? Remember, the spirit of fear does not come from God. Instead, God gave us power and love and a sound mind (see 2 Timothy 1.7). Therefore, you need to ask the Lord Jesus to close the door that you opened.

How is this done? First you need to recognize you have sinned. Most fear, anxiety, and worry come through the sin of not trusting God.

Second, confession is necessary. Face yourself. Tell

God. And then, if possible, confess to someone close to you.

When all this is done, you may then claim the precious promises for cleansing. You will instantly be freed from the bondage of Satan.

Worry is a demon – fear of demons comes from demons themselves. As children of God, we have nothing to fear. He who is in us is much stronger than he who is against us.

'And he asked them, "Why were you so fearful? Don't you even yet have confidence in me?" ' (Mark 4.40 TLB).

The seed among the thorns represents those who listen and believe God's word but whose faith afterwards is choked out by worry and riches and the responsibilities and pleasures of life . . .' (Luke 8.14 TLB).

May we worry? We have a whole Bible as our guide, Jesus Christ as our living Saviour who loves us, and heaven as our future.

Worry does not empty tomorrow of its sorrow, it empties today of its strength. It does not enable us to escape evil. It makes us unfit to face evil when it comes. It is the interest you pay on trouble before it comes.

Worry is a cycle of inefficient thoughts whirling around a centre of fear.

A Higher Wisdom

'Where there is no vision, the people perish.'
Proverbs 29.18 KJV

How we need to have good vision in this time when all is so dark. The Holy Spirit gives us good eyes, that we may see God's plan in the midst of all the chaos of this time.

In 1 Corinthians 1 and 2, Paul talks about the 'foolishness' of God and the 'wisdom' of the wise. These are two realms we need to recognize. The wisdom of the wise is all we can grasp with our logical thinking, with our brains. The 'foolishness' of God, the greatest wisdom, we can only touch with our faith knowledge. The Holy Spirit teaches us to lift up the wisdom of the wise to the height of the foolishness of God, and then we get the vision.

When people do not know the Lord and are not born into the family of God, they cannot see or understand the kingdom of God, because they have only their logical thinking, the use of their brains. And when you try to bring the foolishness of God under the criticism of the wisdom of the wise, then you may end up with a theology that says, 'God is dead.'

We live in an age when one of the signs of the end time which Daniel gave is becoming very clear: '. . . knowledge shall increase' (Daniel 12.4 RSV). Some people expect that in the coming ten years the sum total of human knowledge will be doubled.

It is such a great danger when only our logical thinking gives us guidance. It may become a weapon in the hands of the antichrist. I experienced that personally once at a congress of communists in Ravensbrück. I had heard that a reunion of ex-prisoners was to be held, and I had hoped to find friends there with whom I had suffered. Instead, forty thousand communists were present.

I listened to their talks, and such darkness fell upon me that when I returned to West Germany, I felt that I had no message with me. The Lord liberated me totally, and I received a strong message from Him. But there I saw how dangerous it is to be permanently in the atmosphere of the wisdom of the wise without any knowledge of the foolishness of God, which is the highest wisdom.

Earthly wisdom is not something that is wrong in itself. We belong to the Lord one hundred per cent, heart and mind. When we have surrendered both to Him, He will show us how to use that wisdom. I remember that when I was a watchmaker with my father, he once said: 'My name is on the shop, but really God's name should be there, because I am a watchmaker by the grace of God.'

Sometimes when we could not find what was wrong with a watch, we prayed that the Lord would show it to us. And Father and I both had the joyful experience that in our dreams in the night the Lord showed us the fault in a watch. When it happened with me, I went down to the workshop and looked to see if my dream was true. I always found that it was. Yes, there is nothing too great for God's power, nothing too small for His love.

When I worked in Vietnam, a doctor came to me when I had a bad case of enteritis. First he prayed with me and claimed victory over the sickness that tried to keep me away from the important work I had to do there. After that, he gave me some very good medicine. I saw that this man knew both the wisdom of the wise and the foolishness of God.

A space traveller once said: 'I was very high up in space, but I never saw God.' That man knew only the wisdom of the wise. We who belong to Jesus can find the wisdom of God, which may be foolishness in the eye of the world, but for us it is a great power to find the way through this dark time we are now experiencing. James tells us where we can find that power: 'If any of you lacks wisdom, let him ask God, who gives to all men generously and without reproaching, and it will be given him. But let him ask in faith, with no doubting' (James 1.5,6 RSV).

Only on earth are there those who do not believe in God. Even though the powers of evil lead men astray and keep them in darkness and unbelief, yet they themselves believe in God and tremble, for they know that on the Lord's Day, judgment awaits them.

Unfolding God's Love Letter

> 'All scripture is inspired by God and profitable for
> teaching, for reproof, for correction, and for training
> in righteousness, that the man of God may be
> complete, equipped for every good work.'
>
> 2 Timothy 3.16,17 RSV

Reading the Bible is the best way to come to know
the Lord Jesus, and yet many times it can be difficult.
A good Dutch friend gave me some very practical
advice on how to study the Word.

'Once the Bible was a closed book to me, but now
it has come alive. I am longing to receive more of its
treasures. I have been given victory over my sins, and
my life has become happier. You may be in the same
position I was in. Perhaps you reached out for the
Bible when you gave your life to Christ. For a while
it was interesting, but then you stopped reading, and
now you are discouraged and do not try to read any
more.

'Are you longing to know the Bible? I believe I have
found a good method for Bible study. The first thing
you must do to study the Bible is to realize that the
Bible is God's book, His love letter to you. If you
know that you are in contact with God through faith
in the forgiveness of your sins by Jesus Christ, then
the Bible can become a living book for you, full of

rich treasures. It is only with this realization that you can truly understand the Bible.

'Next you must ask God for His help and believe that He hears your prayer.

'Now take your Bible and choose a book to study. Let us start with the Gospel of John, chapter 1, verses 1–14.

'Ask yourself, "What is the most beautiful verse and why is this so?" In John, I believe verse 12 is the most beautiful: "But as many as received him, to them gave he power to become the sons of God, even to them that believe on his name." (KJV).

'I find this beautiful because there is no other condition which is required to become a child of God than faith.

'Now look through the passage again and consider the question, "Is there a promise for me in this section?" A young man once said to me after he studied this question, "I have received a new Bible, for I have found Christ in it."

'A girl in a Bible study camp once found a wonderful promise in verse 9: He "lighteth every man." This made her very happy, she told me with shining eyes, because she knew now that God seeks contact with every person from the beginning of his life.

'Next, examine the passage to see if there is a warning in it. I find in verse 11: "his own received him not." This is a warning that we may pass on to others, to all with whom we have an opportunity to speak of Jesus Christ. Not receiving Him means to go into eternity unsaved.

'The last question to ask is, "Did a prayer come into my heart while I was reading this passage?" I wanted to pray while I was reading verse 4: "Lord, grant that many may see that light and commit themselves to You.''

'Is Bible study difficult? No. It just requires some time and prayer. Try to get some friends together, and use this method of Bible study. If you read your Bible, I am sure that you will experience its power in your life.'

My friend is right; Bible study is not difficult. Understanding the Bible does not depend upon the wisdom of your mind or mine. We should never use the standards of our own reason when we read the Scriptures.

If only we would accept the Bible in a simple, child-like way, as the Word of God, the Word that teaches us about the foolishness of God which is wiser than the wisdom of men, and the love of God that passes all understanding. How greatly it would change our lives; we would begin to see things in the right perspective. We need never fear to trust in the Word, because the Bible is absolutely reliable.

I will tell you some reasons why I believe that the Bible is inspired. First of all, it says so! '. . . holy men of God spake as they were moved by the Holy Ghost' (2 Peter 1.21 kjv).

I also look at the effect it has had on all who believe and follow it. How could it have had so much influence without the Holy Spirit? Also, even though some of the books were written more than two thousand years apart, the writers agree.

Against human nature, the authors do not offer any excuse for their own faults or sins. They record the most harrowing scenes that affected them very much, yet they never express one word of emotion. The Holy Spirit wanted the facts recorded and not their feelings about the facts.

How wonderful to have a love letter from God! He took the time to write it; shouldn't we take more time to read it?

God writes with a pen that never blots, speaks with a tongue that never slips, and acts with a hand that never fails.

The promises in the Bible are our budget. They are all made payable to us through Jesus Christ and can be claimed by faith. This is our victory, our faith.

Don't worry about what you do not understand of the Bible. Worry about what you do understand but do not live by.

To get the most from your Bible, read it with your ears open.

Let Scripture speak. Paul appealed to the Scriptures, even though the people who listened did not believe.

The Protection of the Most High

'Trust in the LORD with all your heart,
And do not lean on your own understanding.
In all your ways acknowledge Him,
And He will make your paths straight'

Proverbs 3.5,6 NASB

Many people came to know and trust the Lord during World War II. One was an Englishman who was held in a German prison camp for a long period of time.

One day he read Psalm 91:

He who dwells in the shelter of the Most High
Will abide in the shadow of the Almighty.
I will say to the LORD, 'My refuge and my fortress,
My God, in whom I trust!'

For you have made the LORD, my refuge,
Even the Most High, your dwelling place.
No evil will befall you,
Nor will any plague come near your tent.
For He will give His angels charge concerning you,
To guard you in all your ways (vv. 1,2,9–11 NASB).

'Father in heaven,' he prayed, 'I see all these men dying around me, one after the other. Will I also have to die here? I am still young and I very much want to work in Your kingdom here on earth.'

He received this answer: 'Rely on what you have just read and go home!'

Trusting in the Lord, he got up and walked into the corridor toward the gate. A guard called out, 'Prisoner, where are you going?'

'I am under the protection of the Most High,' he replied. The guard came to attention and let him pass, for Adolf Hitler was known as 'the Most High.'

He came to the gate, where a group of guards stood. They commanded him to stop and asked where he was going.

'I am under the protection of the Most High.' All the guards stood at attention as he walked out the gate.

The English officer made his way through the German countryside and eventually reached England, where he told how he had made his escape.

He was the only one to come out of that prison alive.

Never be afraid to trust an unknown future to a known God.

God has a telescopic and a microscopic interest in us: The whole world is in His hands; the hairs of our head are numbered.

Christ's limitless resources meet our endless needs.

Outside His Boundaries

> '*Stay always within the boundaries where God's love can reach and bless you . . .*'
>
> Jude 21 TLB

During the war I had an experience that reminded me how important it is to stay in the centre of God's will – the safest place in the world.

After I came home from Ravensbrück, a man I did not know came to see me one day. He showed me a paper and said that a friend of his was in prison and that his life was in danger.

'You know the governor of that prison,' he said. 'He is a good Hollander and he is on our side. Will you come and introduce me to him, give him this paper, and ask him to release my friend?'

'I don't think I know that governor,' I told him, 'but I am willing to come with you. Let us pray first, however, that the Lord may protect us.'

On bikes without tyres we went to the prison and rang the bell. When the guard opened the door, I asked to speak to the governor. As the door closed behind us, I began to feel uncomfortable. When I saw the governor I knew I had never met him before.

'May I talk with you just a moment?' I asked.

He took us down a corridor till we were in the centre of the prison. I gave the paper to him. He looked at it, then said, 'Wait a minute. I'll call the

Gestapo to see whether or not this request can be granted.'

My heart sank. Had my companion mistaken me for someone else?

'No, no, let me just talk with you a moment,' I said. But he left.

The governor was gone for perhaps five minutes. While we waited, I recognized the prison smell I knew so well. I heard a man pounding on the door of his cell, crying, 'Let me go! I want to get out of here! Open the door!'

This was all too familiar to me; I began to tremble. Could my liberty have been so short? A terrible fear came over me, a fear I had not felt during all the time I was in Ravensbrück.

The governor returned and led us to his office. When he had shut the door, he turned to me and said, 'Are you an underground worker? How stupid you are! Look at this paper. There are three very big errors in it.'

I knew it was not my fault, but I listened to his reprimand with joy; he was telling me that he was an underground worker and a good Dutchman, so I need not fear anything.

'If I did what you ask,' he continued. 'I would have to go underground at once with all my helpers. I intend to stay here and help until the last day of the war.'

Then he looked at me and sighed. 'I will tell you how you can get this young man free.'

'Tell this man, please,' I said, gesturing toward my companion. While I listened to their voices, the room whirled around me. My heartbeat became normal again only when I was safely out of the prison.

'You looked so scared,' my companion said as we

were walking out. 'I was told you were never afraid. You looked like a ghost.'

Yes, I had been afraid. Was I the same Corrie ten Boom who stood in pitch dark in the concentration camp, comforting my friends as they went to their deaths?

I was the same Corrie ten Boom. But in the concentration camp I was in the place where God had called me, and He was my strength. Here I was not in His will, and without Him I was nothing – I was stupid, weak, and helpless.

After this incident my friends forbade me to do any more underground work. I agreed.

On the last day of the war, the prison governor released eighteen prisoners who were to be shot that day. He and all the guards who had helped him escaped in the nick of time.

There is no right way to do a wrong thing.

'I will all the more gladly boast of my weaknesses, that the power of Christ may rest upon me' (2 Corinthians 12.9 RSV).

We will see more and more that we are chosen not because of our ability, but because of His power that will be demonstrated in our not being able.

The Fullness of the Spirit

> 'He who believes in me . . . out of his heart shall flow rivers of living water . . . this he said about the Spirit, which those who believed in him were to receive.'
>
> John 7.38 RSV

We can expect Jesus' coming very soon, and we must be ready. As the wise virgins had oil in their lamps, so we have to be filled with the Holy Spirit. The wise virgins refused to give half of their oil to the foolish virgins, because they knew that half a portion was not sufficient to reach the house of celebration and to light their lamps during the marriage feast. So we must have our full portion of the Holy Spirit to be ready for Jesus' coming.

What joy it is that He is willing to fill our hearts like a light is ready to fill a room that is open to its brightness. Let us only offer Him a clean house. That is possible when we bring all our unconfessed sins to the Lord and claim 1 John 1.7, the cleansing by the blood of Jesus.

Being filled with the Spirit is not so much a question of striving but of surrendering to Him who will keep you steadfast in the faith to the end, so that when His day comes, you need fear no condemnation (see 1 Corinthians 1.8).

Let us not underestimate the power and work of

the Holy Spirit. The Word of God tells us: 'Ye must be born again . . . born of the Spirit' (John 3.7,8 κjv). To be 'born again' means not only our turning to God, but God's putting His Spirit within us to be the new life in our souls, thus making us children of God.

I have discovered three steps in being born of the Holy Spirit: receive, recognize, and rely.

Receive: In seeking this new life, your part is to turn from sin to God, claim your union with the Saviour who died and rose again for you, and ask for and receive the Holy Spirit.

Jesus' part is to put all the past under His blood and to breathe into your heart His Holy Spirit to cause you to know Him as a personal Saviour. Therefore ask, and by faith, receive the Holy Spirit, because God, who cannot fail, promises to give to all those who ask. Prove your faith by giving thanks to God and by bearing witness to men of the covenant made with God.

Recognize: Recognize that the Holy Spirit is within you, and obey Him in all things. Remember you have opened your heart to a divine Person, the third Person of the Trinity, who has come to 'lead you into all truth.' Beware of forgetting your contract with God. God must have first place in your heart and life. Do not wait for 'feelings,' but expect the Holy Spirit to teach you, convict you of sin, and transform you until you are well-pleasing in His sight.

Rely: Rely upon the Holy Spirit within you to give you victory over every temptation of the devil and make you more than conqueror. As you read God's Word, ask Him especially to speak some promise to your heart, witnessing that the Holy Spirit has come to you: thus you will be ready to meet the tempter with the Sword of the Spirit. Rely on the Holy Spirit for everything. Long for anything that is God's will for you, and trust Him to work in you.

'I tell you, Ask, and it will be given you; seek, and you will find; knock and it will be opened to you. . . . What father among you, if his son asks for a fish, will instead of a fish give him a serpent . . .? If you then, who are evil, know how to give good gifts to your children, how much more will your heavenly Father give the Holy Spirit to those who ask him!' (Luke 11.9,11,13 RSV).

Guilt never heals; its purpose is only to lead us to the Healer.

When temptation knocks at the door, I ask Jesus to open the door. That is very safe.

There is a hunger in our heart that is never satisfied, but by Jesus. Do you feel lonesome, hungry? Do you have problems that you can't solve? Do you feel chased and you don't see a way out? Come to Him.

We can't solve problems for others, but we can introduce them to the Lord.

Trust and Obey

'Let nothing move you as you busy yourselves in the Lord's work. Be [assured] that nothing you do for him is ever lost or ever wasted.'

1 Corinthians 15.58 PHILLIPS

Did you testify to your faith this week? The Lord used you. Did you get discouraged? Perhaps you will not see it here, but in heaven you will see how the Lord has used you. Trust and obey.

I remember that when I worked in Russia, there was a time when I did not have many opportunities to witness. But in the hotel were two American people who always tried to sit at our table. How they loved to hear us talk about the Lord Jesus. Later, we lost their address, and so I lost contact with them. What a joy when a year later I received a letter from the lady who told me, 'What a lot my husband and I learned through the conversations at the hotel dining-room table in Moscow. My husband died last month, and he knew that his sins were forgiven through Jesus Christ. God used you to show us the way.'

When you trust and obey, the Lord does the job. Hallelujah!

No one can trust God who does not obey God. Obedience is

the root of confidence. For Jesus, trusting went quite without saying, because for Him obedience went without saying.

Obedience is doing no less than we are asked. Trust is doing no more than we are asked.

Don't bother to give God instructions; just report for duty.

'From that city many of the Samaritans believed in Him because of the word of the woman who testified . . .' (John 4.39 NASB).

Times of Tribulation

'We pray that you will be strengthened from God's glorious power, so that you may be able to pass through any experience and endure it with joy.'
Colossians 1.11 PHILLIPS

A girl asked me, 'How can I become strong enough to withstand tribulation?' My answer was, 'Search the Scriptures! The Bible gives many powerful and practical texts, and it is good to learn them by heart.'

A big part of the body of Christ is suffering tribulation now, and it is good to be prepared. Before the Lord Jesus comes to make everything new, a time will come when Christians will experience what Jesus said: 'In the world ye shall have tribulation: but be of good cheer; I have overcome the world' (John 16.33 KJV).

God develops spiritual power in our lives through the pressures of hard places.

Praise lifts your eyes from the battle to the victory, for Christ is already Victor in your heart that you might have His victory in your life.

How do I manage a difficulty? Well, at first I try to walk past it. If that does not help, I try to climb over it; and when I cannot climb over it, to crawl underneath. And when that is not possible I go straight through — God and I!

Search the Bible for promises you can use in days of persecution and tribulation. Learn the promises by heart.

We mutter and flutter, we fume and we spurt.
We mumble and grumble, our feelings get hurt.
We can't understand things, our vision gets dim,
When all that we need is a moment with Him.

Surrender

'. . . do not be anxious beforehand what you are to say; but say whatever is given you in that hour, for it is not you who speak, but the Holy Spirit'

(Mark 13.11 RSV).

'Has the Lord as much delight in burnt offerings and sacrifices
As in obeying the voice of the Lord?
Behold, to obey is better than sacrifice . . .'
(1 Samuel 15.22 NASB).

Surrender to the Lord is not a tremendous sacrifice, not an agonizing performance; it is the most sensible thing you can do.

Peter said, 'No, Lord!' But he had to learn that one cannot say no while saying Lord, and that one cannot say Lord while saying no.

'Now to him who is able to keep you from falling and to present you before his glory without fault and with unspeak-

able joy, to the only God, our saviour, be glory and majesty, power and authority, through Jesus Christ our Lord, before time was, now, and in all ages to come, amen' (Jude 24,25 PHILLIPS).

The greatest sin for a sinner is to refuse Jesus. The greatest sin for a Christian is to refuse the fullness of the Holy Spirit.

'What does it cost to be a Christian?' someone asked Henry Drummond. His reply was, 'The entrance fee is nothing, but the annual subscription is everything.'

I'll Go Where You Want Me to Go, Dear Lord . . .*

'God is able to make all grace abound toward you; that ye, always having all sufficiency in all things, may abound to every good work.'

2 Corinthians 9.8 KJV

I had spoken that Sunday morning in a church in Copenhagen, Denmark, urging the people to present their bodies as living sacrifices to the Lord. I had said that even though I was an old woman I wanted to give myself completely to Jesus and do whatever He wanted me to do, go wherever He wanted me to go – even if it meant dying.

After church time, two young nurses approached me. They invited me up to their apartment to have a cup of coffee. I was very tired. At almost eighty years of age I found that standing on my feet for long periods of time was beginning to be exhausting. The cup of coffee sounded good, so I accepted their invitation.

But I was not prepared for the walk to their apartment. Many of the houses in Copenhagen are old, high houses with no lifts. The nurses lived on

*From *Tramp for the Lord*, pp. 141–143, copyright © 1974 by Corrie ten Boom and Jamie Buckingham. All rights reserved. Used by permission of Hodder & Stoughton.

the tenth floor of such a house, and we had to walk up the steps.

'Oh Lord,' I complained as I looked up at the high building, 'I do not think I can make it.' But the nurses wanted me to come up so badly that I consented to try.

By the time we reached the fifth floor my heart was pounding wildly and my legs were so tired I thought they could not take another step. In the corridor of the fifth floor I saw a chair and pleaded with the Lord, 'Lord, let me stay here a time while the nurses go on up the stairs. My heart is so unhappy.'

The nurses waited patiently as I collapsed into the chair, resting. 'Why, O Lord, must I have this stair-climbing after this busy day of speaking?'

Then I heard God's voice, even louder than my pounding heart, 'Because a great blessing is awaiting you, a work which will give joy to the angels.'

I looked up at the steps, towering above me and almost disappearing into the clouds. Perhaps I am leaving this earth to go to heaven, I thought. Surely that will give joy to the angels. I tried to count the steps. It seemed there were at least one hundred more to climb. However, if God said that the work would give joy to the angels, then I had to go. I rose from my chair and once again started trudging up the long flight of stairs, one nurse in front of me, the other behind me.

We finally reached the apartment on the tenth floor, and on entering I found a room with a simple lunch already prepared on the table. Serving the lunch were the mother and father of one of the girls.

I knew there was only a short time and also knew that a blessing of some kind was awaiting us. So without many introductions, I started asking . . . questions.

'Tell me,' I asked the nurse's mother, 'is it long ago that you found Jesus as your Saviour?'

'I have never met Him,' she said, surprised at my question.

'Are you willing to come to Him? He loves you. I have travelled in more than sixty countries and have never found anyone who said they were sorry they had given their hearts to Jesus. You will not be sorry, either.'

Then I opened my Bible and pointed out the verses about salvation. She listened intently. Then I asked them, 'Shall we now talk with the Lord?'

I prayed, then the two nurses prayed, and finally the mother folded her hands and said, 'Lord Jesus, I know already much about You. I have read much in the Bible, but now I pray You to come into my heart. I need cleansing and salvation. I know that You died at the cross for the sins of the whole world and also for my sins. Please, Lord, come into my heart and make me a child of God. Amen.'

I looked up and saw tears of joy on the face of the young nurse. She and her friend had prayed so much for her parents and now the answer was given. I turned and looked at the father, who had sat quietly through all this.

'What about you?' I asked him.

'I have never made such a decision for Jesus Christ, either,' he said seriously. 'But I have listened to all you have told my wife and now I know the way. I, too, would like to pray that Jesus will save me.'

He bowed his head and from his lips poured a joyful but very sincere prayer as he gave his life to Jesus Christ. Suddenly, the room was filled with great

44

rejoicing and I realized the angels had come down and were standing around, singing praises unto God.

'Thank You, Lord,' I prayed as I walked down the long steps, 'for making me walk up all these steps. And next time, Lord, help Corrie ten Boom listen to her own sermon about being willing to go anywhere You tell me to go – even up ten flights of stairs.'

When God's hand is on you, you run much quicker than you are able.

Find out where you can render a service, and then render it. The rest is up to the Lord.

The Good Fight

> *'For just as the sufferings of Christ are ours in abundance, so also our comfort is abundant through Christ.'*
>
> 2 Corinthians 1.5 NASB

Often I have heard people say, 'How good God is. We prayed that it would not rain for our church picnic, and look at this lovely weather!' Yes, God is good when He sends good weather. But God was also good when He allowed my sister Betsie to starve to death before my eyes in the German concentration camp.

I remember one occasion when I was very discouraged there. Everything around us was dark, and there was darkness in my heart. I remember telling Betsie that I thought God had forgotten us.

'No, Corrie,' said Betsie, 'He has not forgotten us. Remember His Word: "For as the heavens are high above the earth, so great is his steadfast love towards those who fear him . . ." ' (Psalm 103.11 KJV).

The Lord in His love accepts us as we are, and if we are obeying Him, He will work through us, whatever our circumstances.

I was very moved when in Russia I met a woman who was totally dedicated to typing out Christian books on her typewriter. She was paralysed – only one finger could be moved. She was in bed, and an old typewriter stood in front of her bed on a small table. Yet she had typed out many Christian books. She was very gifted and had read a great number of books. Among many others, she had translated my books and given them to people.

Very often we say that we have no time and strength to work for the Lord. I was ashamed when I saw this woman. Able to move only one finger, she spent many hours a day typing to spread the gospel. The Lord wants to use everybody, if only we will be obedient and are in the centre of His will.

Perhaps you think, 'I don't have enough faith.' Hudson Taylor, the great missionary to China, said, 'It is not a great faith that we need, but faith in a great God.' Jesus said that even if our faith is as small as a mustard seed, we can move mountains.

When the gaoler at Philippi asked Paul and Silas, 'What must I do to be saved?' they answered, 'Believe on the Lord Jesus Christ, and thou shalt be saved . . .' (Acts 16.30,31 KJV). When you take this step you become a child of God; you are on the Lord's side at the very moment you enter through the door of faith.

This is the great beginning of the fight of faith, and we need the armour of God so that we may stand our ground even when we have come to a standstill. But it is a fight of victory; the Lord throws open wide the door of faith's treasure-house of plenty and bids us enter and take with boldness.

God bless you. There is an ocean of God's love available through the Holy Spirit (see Romans 5.5). There is plenty for everyone. May God grant you never to doubt that victorious love – whatever the circumstances.

Friendship

Witnessing for Christ is the greatest work in the world. It is the most honouring to Christ, the most joyful to the Christian, the most beneficial in its blessed effect to those who are won.

If you would serve others you must be ready to be saved by others, that is, to be admonished and set right by others.

Be united with other Christians. A wall with loose bricks is no good. The bricks must be cemented together.

The glory of friendship is not the outstretched hand, nor the kindly smile, nor the joy of companionship; it is the spiritual inspiration that comes to one when he discovers that someone else believes in him and is willing to trust him with his friendship.

To speak to God on behalf of man is probably the highest service any of us can render. The next is to speak to men in the name of Jesus. Either is possible, through His grace.

Everlasting Life*

> Nothing 'shall be able to separate us from the love of
> God, which is in Christ Jesus our Lord.'
>
> Romans 8.39 KJV

As far astern as one could go on the deck of a freighter,
I found a quiet spot where I could be delightfully
alone.

I leaned on the rail and gazed at the silver wake left
by our boat on the surface of the sea. Dolphins were
leaping out of the water. Seven seagulls were circling
around the ship. They would follow us faithfully until
land was again within sight.

I mused.

What a tiny cockle-shell our vessel is on the
immensity of the sea!

What a minute, insignificant, and temporal creature
I am! Between my birth and my death I am permitted
to live on this earth for some time and after that . . .
eternity.

Where am I exactly?

Here I am aboard a tiny ship, and deep, deep under
me is the sea, full of the mysterious life of marine
animals. Above me is the infinite sky, out of which a
tempest might come to wreck this little vessel. Around

*From *Amazing Love* by Corrie ten Boom, pp. 111–112. Copyright
© 1957 Christian Literature Crusade, London. Used by permission.

me is the endless sea, in which so many people have drowned.

Where, exactly, am I?

I live in a world where demons rule, where wars are waged, where millions of people are starving, where cities are turned into ruins in many parts of [the world]; where atom bombs are surpassed in destructive power by hydrogen bombs.

Exactly where am I?

I am in a world which God so loved, 'that he gave his only begotten Son, that whosoever believeth in him, should not perish, but have everlasting life' (John 3.16 KJV).

I am on an earth where soon He shall come, even He who has promised, 'Behold, I make all things new' (Revelation 21.5 KJV).

One day the earth, this beautiful earth, 'shall be filled with the knowledge of the glory of the LORD, as the waters cover the sea' (Habakkuk 2.14 KJV).

Where am I exactly?

Already, at this moment, I am in Him.

And underneath me are His eternal arms.

Prayer

What wings are to a bird and sails to a ship, is prayer to the soul.

As a camel kneels before his master to have him remove his burden at the end of the day, so kneel each night and let the Master take your burden.

We possess a divine artillery that silences the enemy and inflicts upon him the damage he would inflict upon us.

Is prayer your steering wheel or your spare tyre?

A disconnected mature Christian is less fruitful than a connected babe in Christ.

A home is like a solar system: The centre, the great sun, holds the system together. Make Jesus your centre!

Red Cap 42

*'Come unto me, all ye that labour and are heavy laden
and I will give you rest.'*

Matthew 11.28 KJV

Corporate prayer is a mighty weapon. I often experienced this in the concentration camp. It drives
demons away. Of the many prayer groups I have
known in America, the prayer group of Red Cap 42
was a remarkable one. He was a black man whom I
met during my travelling days at his stand in Grand
Central Station, New York.

The doors to the tracks were opened only ten
minutes before the trains left. The Red Caps had the
keys to these doors. Three times a week at noon,
Ralston Crosby Young, Red Cap 42, gathered his
friends and a few newcomers – people from all walks
of society – in front of one of these doors. When all
were present, he opened the door and preceded them
down the stairs to an empty train at the underground
platform. They sat down in a compartment, and
Ralston said a short prayer and read a Bible portion.
Then he told something about his life and conversion
and invited others to say a few words. Some of them
told about their difficulties, others of Christ's victories
in their lives, and then many prayed in turn, short
and powerful prayers.

It was dark in the compartment and on the platform,

for the lights were turned on only when the train left. Here these people were gathered in the heart of New York City, each one with his or her cares and struggles and their longing to serve Christ. Together they sought their strength in prayer. Their meeting time was half-way between their working hours. Perhaps it was nothing special they were discussing, but together these people were close to God for a while.

A little later, travellers flooded onto the platform and each one went to his or her office, school, factory, or wherever the work was waiting. Red Cap 42 took the luggage of an old lady who did not know the way and was looking anxiously around her. She asked him something, and then I heard him answer: 'Just pray!'

Say, did you pray today? Did you tell everything to God? He loves you and understands you. There is nothing too great for His power; there is nothing too small for His love.

Little is much if God is in it; man's busiest day is not worth God's minute.

Christic in You

> *'How I long for [you] to experience the wealth of
> conviction which is brought by understanding – that
> [you] may come to know more fully God's great
> secret, Christ himself!'*
>
> Colossians 2.2 PHILLIPS

A millionaire once prayed at every meeting of his
church for the fullness of the Holy Spirit. Someone
said to him, 'Do you know what that means? The
Holy Spirit must also come into your wallet!'

For four weeks the man would not pray for the
fullness of the Holy Spirit. But he finally realized that
his money was not making him happy, fulfilled, or at
peace. After he asked again to receive the Holy Spirit,
the Lord directed the man to give money to do His
work; but, of course, the man soon found his life to
be even richer because he had allowed the Spirit to
take control.

Hudson Taylor said, 'God gives the Holy Spirit not
to those who long for Him, not to those who pray for
Him, and not to those who desire to be filled always;
but He does give the Holy Spirit to them that obey
Him.' Indeed, the fullness of the Holy Spirit means to
lose your life for Christ's sake (see Luke 9.24), and in
that way to gain it in its fullest.

Some people think that I must be a very noble
Corrie ten Boom to have been able to work in

Germany and to forgive those who were very cruel to my family, even causing the deaths of some of them. But they do not understand that I, without Jesus Christ, could not love and help the German people. When Jesus tells us to love our enemies, He provides the love that He asks from us. Until we have loved our enemies, we have not tapped that love of which Jesus speaks. This means more than simply trying your hardest to be good. The truth is that God longs to give us the riches of His glory (see Ephesians 1.18). He is the only One from whom we can receive the power we need to be all that He wants us to be.

Jesus knocks at the door of our hearts, and when we open, He fills us with His joy, the fullness of the Holy Spirit, and the love of God.

Rebellion against the Holy Spirit makes a vacuum that the devil likes to fill.

Put yourself, your ability, your money at God's disposal. He can do so much more with it than you can.

What have you done today that only a Christian would have done?

He Brought the Word, Jesus*

'He must increase, but I must decrease.'

John 3.30 KJV

The Indian Christian, the Sadhu Sundar Singh, was once asked if he was influenced by the honour his friends gave him.

He said, 'When Jesus entered Jerusalem, many people spread their clothing and palm branches on the street to honour the Lord.' Jesus was riding, as the prophets foretold, on a donkey. In this way the feet of Jesus did not touch the street adorned with clothes and branches, but instead the donkey walked over them. 'It would have been very stupid of the donkey if she had imagined that she was very important. It was not for her that the people threw their clothes on the streets.'

Stupid are those who spread the good news of Jesus and expect to receive glory themselves. The glory should go to Jesus.

The more people came to this godly man after his meetings, the more the Sadhu Sundar Singh withdrew from the crowd, to be in the silence where God spoke to him.

*From the July 8th entry in *Each New Day*, copyright © 1977 by Corrie ten Boom. Used by permission of Kingsway Publications.

No sensation. No show.
He brought them the living Word, Jesus.

Churches do not lack great scholars and great minds, they lack men and women who can and will be channels for the power of God.

> *A vision without a task, makes a visionary,*
> *A task with a vision, makes a missionary.*

If you have some time on your hands, spend part of it on your knees.

God's Riches

'. . . God shall supply all your needs according to His riches in glory in Christ Jesus.'
Philippians 4.19 NASB

When the Bible writers describe our riches in Jesus Christ, they often use words starting with 'un': joy unspeakable (see 1 Peter 1.8), unsearchable riches (see Ephesians 3.8), and unspeakable gifts (see 2 Corinthians 9.15). It seems as if they cannot find words to show the abundance the Lord gives us.

I think the reason is that the boundless resources of God's promises are celestial. They are earthly reproductions of heavenly riches in Jesus Christ, and they are ours under every circumstance.

All of His riches are for us – not to admire, but to take and keep. The antichrist is marching on and organizing his army over the whole world, but we stand on the Lord's side and may accept all His promises.

Too often we are like people who stand in front of the show window of a jewellery store. We admire the beautiful watches, rings, and bracelets, but we do not go in and pay the price in order to possess them. We just walk away! It is through Jesus that God's greatest and most precious promises have become available to us.

In my book *Plenty for Everyone*, I tell of a parable by

F. B. Meyer which describes a rich palace that is open to everyone who belongs to the Lord Jesus. Jesus is the door to the palace, and when we put our hands into His, He leads us from room to room.

The first room: REBIRTH
'... Except a man be born again, he cannot enter into the kingdom of God' (John 3.3 KJV).

The second room: ASSURANCE OF SALVATION
'You that believe on the name of the Son of God ... may know that ye have eternal life' (John 5.13 KJV).

The third room: SURRENDERED WILL
'I delight to do thy will, O my God ...' (Psalm 40.8 KJV). Sometimes it seems so hard that we have to pray, 'Lord, make me willing to surrender my will.'

The fourth room: TOTAL SURRENDER
'The price was in fact the life blood of Christ ...' (1 Peter 1.19 PHILLIPS).

The fifth room: THE FULLNESS OF THE HOLY SPIRIT
'... be filled with the Spirit' (Ephesians 5.18 KJV). Have you got the Holy Spirit? Has the Holy Spirit got you? Some people think the Spirit is for the spiritual aristocracy. But He is for every child of God.

The sixth room: ABIDING IN CHRIST
'... abide in him; that when he shall appear, we may have confidence, and not be ashamed before him at his coming' (1 John 2.28 KJV).

The seventh room: VICTORY OVER SIN

'Thanks be to God, which giveth us the victory through our Lord Jesus Christ' (1 Corinthians 15.57 KJV). Every child of God is to be an overcomer.

The eighth room: HEART'S REST

'. . . we . . . do not cease to pray for you, and desire that you might be filled with the knowledge of his will in all wisdom and spiritual understanding' (Colossians, 1.9 KJV). Rest in the Lord is independent of our external circumstances: It is a trusting, triumphant relationship with the Lord Himself.

If we live only in the first room, rebirth, we can be happy to realize that we are saved, but it is only the beginning. There is so much more available. The Bible tells us that there is a kingdom to build.

When Jesus reigns in our hearts, we have all the power necessary to build the kingdom. When we live like beggars, we are unhappy and do not enjoy the riches to which we have a legal right. Give Him the chance to multiply what He gives. Every child of God can live in all the rooms . . . for Jesus is alive and He is the door.

'For I am confident of this very thing, that He who began a good work in you will perfect it until the day of Christ Jesus' (Philippians 1.6 NASB).

Apart From Him, I Can Do Nothing*

> 'As the branch cannot bear fruit of itself, except it
> abide in the vine; no more can ye, except ye abide in
> me.'
>
> John 15.4 KJV

It is so tiring to hold the edge of my bed during the
rolling of the ship that I fasten myself with a rope to
my mattress. I am the only passenger on board the
freighter, and I must share my cabin with the gyrocompass. I am a bad sailor and find sea travel a
tribulation. Suddenly a huge wave hurls against the
ship and I hear a strange sound. The gyrocompass
whistles night and day, but now it is broken and the
noise is peculiar. One of the engineers comes to
repair it.

'Is this a bad storm?' I ask.

'Why, no! This is nothing at all. Wait until the wind
force is 14, then we shall really know what rolling is.'

At that moment, as if to contradict his words, a big
wave throws the ship to one side. I hear the breaking
of china, and everything that is not securely fastened
runs from one side of the cabin to the other.

The storm has subsided by next morning, so I climb

*From *Not Good If Detached* by Corrie ten Boom, pp. 33–35.
Copyright © 1957 by Christian Literature Crusade, London. Used
by permission.

up to the bridge and meet the captain. After a chat about the weather, I say, 'Captain, it is Sunday. May we have a church service?'

'What? A church service on my ship? It would be the first in my life!'

'Then,' I reply with a smile, 'it is high time you began, sir.'

'All right. You can use the mess room. I am not opposed to the idea.'

He himself writes on the notice-board that at 11:00 A.M. there will be a church service in the mess room. At the appointed time nobody appears. The cabin boy brings me a cup of coffee. It is a Dutch ship, and the ship's cook knows that an 11:00 A.M. cup of coffee is a tradition.

'Are you going to stay?' I ask the boy. 'I have a very interesting story to tell you.'

'I don't want to hear that nonsense,' he says. 'I will not have anything to do with that Bible and God business.' He feels very cocksure, and leaves me alone.

I never saw so empty a church; just a cup of coffee and myself. I am not at all on fire for the Lord. Were I enthusiastic, I would go to the bridge and say, 'Come along, gentlemen; you must help me to fill the mess room. Send your men and boys.' But I don't do that. I go to my cabin and am very seasick. That is the only thing I can do during the whole week.

Sunday comes around again. I am feeling discouraged and ashamed. . . . 'Lord, I am not a missionary. Send me back to my watchmaking business. I am not worthy to do Your work.'

At that moment I find in my Bible a little piece of paper which I have never seen before. On it is written:

> *Cowardly, wayward, and weak,*
> *I change with the changing sky,*
> *Today so eager and strong,*
> *Tomorrow not caring to try.*
> *But He never gives in,*
> *And we two shall win,*
>   *Jesus and I.*

Instantly I see it! Indeed I am not worthy at all. The branch without the Vine cannot produce fruit, but I can do all things through Christ who gives me strength. The strongest and the weakest branches are worth nothing without the Vine; but connected to it they have the same nature.

I go up to the bridge. 'Captain, it is Sunday. Can we have a church service?'

'Again? In a church as empty as last week?' he asks teasingly.

'No, Captain. Not empty, but full, and you must help me.'

He does, and there are ten men in the mess room. When my sermon is finished the cabin boy says, 'It was not boring at all!'

If God has called you, do not spend time looking over your shoulder to see who is following.

Are You Free?

'If the Son therefore shall make you free, ye shall be free indeed.'

John 8.36 KJV

The reason for our lack of freedom can often be found in our past:

- in a sin we committed
- in forgiveness for and from people with whom we have or had a relationship
- in bondage to wrong people
- in bondage to right people

In a sin we committed

We look at our sins by means of two influences:

(a) Satan is an accuser of the saints (see Rev. 12.10). He shows us our sins and brings us to despair. He tells us that this is the way we are and that there is no hope of change for us.

(b) The Holy Spirit shows us our sins in the blessed floodlight of the finished work at the cross. He tells us Jesus died for these sins and bore the punishment and that He lives and is willing to make us more than conquerors. He cleanses us with His blood and gives us victory. We overcome by the blood of the Lamb and the word of our testimony (see Rev. 12.11). Jesus is the answer, and by the Holy Spirit we are able to close our ears to the accuser.

In forgiveness for and from people with whom we have or had a relationship

I experienced the great miracle that I could forgive the murderers of my loved ones. I claimed Romans 5.5: '. . . the love of God is shed abroad in our hearts by the Holy Ghost . . .' (KJV). That is exactly the promise we must claim to be able to forgive! Never wait for people to ask forgiveness.

In bondage to wrong people

How the enemy will use human channels! The answer is to break the friendship in the power of Jesus Christ. We cannot be ready for His coming when we are not right with God and man.

In bondage to right people

I had to learn this myself. There was a work inspired by my sister Betsie who died in the concentration camp. She had shown me the work I should do after the war. I had to leave that work, and I felt very sad. There came a depression upon me. A sister in the Lord showed me that bondage to someone who had died could be wrong. I was set free in the name of Jesus, and the Lord gave me great peace.

To Prisoners

'In all these things we are more than conquerors through him that loved us.'

Romans 8.37 KJV

In the concentration camp where I was imprisoned many years ago, sometimes bitterness and hatred tried to enter my heart when people were so cruel to my sister and me. Then I learned this prayer, a 'thank you' for Romans 5.5.

'Thank You, Lord Jesus, that You have brought into my heart the love of God through the Holy Spirit, who is given to me. Thank You, Father, that Your love in me is victorious over the bitterness in me and cruelty around me.'

After I prayed it, I experienced the miracle that there was no room for bitterness in my heart any more. Will you learn to pray that prayer too?

If you are a child of God, you have a great task in your position. You are a representative of the Lord Jesus, the King of kings (see 2 Corinthians 5.20). He will use you to win others for Christ. You can't? I can't either, but Jesus can.

The Bible says, '. . . be filled with the Spirit' (Ephesians 5.18 KJV). If you give room in your life to the Holy Spirit, then He can work through you, making you the salt of the earth and a shining light in your prison.

A Garden of the Lord

'*In this work, we work with God, and that means
you are a field under God's cultivation . . .*'
1 Corinthians 3.9 PHILLIPS

When you are a little bit old like I am, then you often
remember very long ago. Perhaps seventy years ago,
we had in Holland among the Christians an expres-
sion that said, 'Don't forget Spurgeon.' Now Spurgeon was an English evangelist of that time, and he
wrote many books. And many times as I am enjoying
my garden, a passage from Spurgeon comes back to
me. It was something of a prayer:

> Oh, to have one's soul under heavenly cultivation,
> no wilderness, but a garden of the Lord, walled
> around by grace, planted by instruction, visited by
> love, weeded by heavenly discipline, and guarded
> by divine power. One's soul thus favoured is
> prepared to yield fruit to the glory of God.

Isn't that beautiful? Have you ever thought of your
life that way – as a garden of the Lord? When we
receive Jesus Christ as our Saviour, then at that
moment each of us becomes a 'garden of the Lord.'
As Spurgeon said, 'not a wilderness, but a field under
heavenly cultivation.'

Of course, there are days without the sun when
nothing seems to be growing! Our spiritual lives are

67

barren – inside we feel that we are a real wilderness. When that attack comes, remember that the battle for the Christian is not against flesh and blood, but against the unseen powers of darkness. It is Satan's work to keep us from the Son – the only place where we can grow. The Bible makes it very clear that Satan will always be our accuser. But he is a liar! Lying is his main business.

God's Word gives us a different promise: 'Where sin abounded, grace did much more abound' (Romans 5.20 KJV). That is what Spurgeon meant when he said that our gardens are walled around by grace!

My garden has a wooden fence around it. The plants accept that their place is inside the fence. They know that is where they can grow. The answer to your and my sin problem is found in 2 Corinthians 12.9: 'My grace is sufficient for you, for my power is made perfect in weakness' (RSV). God's grace in calling us to His Son can never be totally understood in this life, but it can be accepted.

This life has a way of separating us from the Saviour's intensive care. Being self-occupied will kill the soil of our spiritual gardens. Jesus makes it clear that the way of self has to be finished. We must lose our lives for His sake to fully experience His power.

Does that mean that your 'self' has to die? Yes. Many of the flowers in this garden were planted as seeds in the fall. In a way, that seed had to die to give birth to all this beauty!

The Holy Spirit does not tell you that you are strong or that you can do anything or everything if you have positive thinking. That is positive fantasy! The Holy Spirit tells us that we are nothing in ourselves. We are like gloves that are filled with a hand and that hand is the Holy Spirit. The joy is when we surrender to the Lord. He does the job to change our wilderness into His garden, and it is He who will make our lives fruitful in the kingdom. Do not expect the Gardener's full help unless you are fully dependent upon Him.

Oh, to have one's soul under heavenly cultivation, no wilderness, but a garden of the Lord, walled around by grace, planted by instruction, visited by love, weeded by heavenly discipline, and guarded by divine power. One's soul thus favoured is prepared to yield fruit to the glory of God.

Are you praying Spurgeon's prayer?

The health department of a country does its utmost to protect the people against germs and infections. What do we do to protect ourselves and others against moral germs and infections?

> *It may be true what the scoffer says,*
> *that the devil is dead and gone.*
> *But sensible people would like to know*
> *who carries the business on.*

Living a Fruitful Life

'*The fruit of the Spirit is love, joy, peace, longsuffer-ing, gentleness, goodness, faith [fulness], meekness, [self-control].*'

Galatians 5.22,23 KJV

Love is the love of Christ that passes knowledge.

Joy is the joy unspeakable and full of glory.

Peace is the peace that passes all understanding that Jesus promised when He said: 'My peace I give unto you.'

Longsuffering is forgiving – even your enemies, just as Jesus forgave His enemies when He was on the cross.

Gentleness is the reproduction of the gentleness of Jesus.

Goodness is Christ-likeness: a kindly disposition.

Faithfulness: The disciples were not always faithful. At the betrayal of Jesus in the garden they all forsook Him and fled. But when the Holy Spirit came down at Pentecost they all became faithful unto death.

Meekness is not the same as weakness. Nor is it a native fruit of the human heart. It is an exotic fruit of heaven.

Self-control is mastering the appetites and passions, particularly the sensual.

All this fruit can be seen in you, but only when you are in contact with the Vine.

When the Spirit Is Willing, But . . .

'. . . the love of God is shed abroad in our hearts by
the Holy Ghost which is given to us.'

Romans 5.5 KJV

Forty years ago when Betsie and I stood in roll-call in
the concentration camp we often saw people from
other barracks. We never could get close enough to
tell them about the Lord Jesus, but we did pray for
them, because every day many died.

Years later I met one of those ladies we prayed for.
She first sent me her whole life story, and after
reading it I knew that she did not know the One who
could make her whole life new. She came to a meeting
where I was speaking and afterwards called me and
said, 'I did not know that such a thing existed as what
you told about. You must have a great faith.'

'No,' I answered, 'I have not a great faith, but even
though it is only as small as a mustard seed, my
Messiah Jesus has said that it is sufficient. My faith
is in a great God!'

'I wish I had a bit of your joy and peace,' she said.
'I cannot forgive the people who have been so cruel
to me.'

Then I told her she could have joy and peace . . .
that all she had to do was ask Jesus Christ into her
life. After I showed her the way, and prayed with
her, she accepted Jesus as her Lord.

How I love Romans 5.5. I use it often, and I shared it with her. She prayed, 'Thank you, Jesus, for Romans 5.5, that you brought into my heart God's love through the Holy Spirit. Thank you, Father, that your love is victorious over my hatred.'

I knew the Lord would perform that miracle and give her a spirit of forgiveness towards those who took her family away. With that same love you can forgive others, dear friends. Your own love runs out, but God's love is always available. It is an act of your will to use this tremendous love. What a joy!

The Lord opens doors and sets the prisoners free, not only people behind iron doors but also prisoners of sin, of bondage. John 8.36 tells us, 'If the Son therefore shall make you free, ye shall be free indeed (KJV).'

Say, are you really free? If not, Jesus can liberate you. Lay your weak hand in His strong hand. He has said, 'Come unto me all who are heavy laden. I will give you rest.'

There are moments when I am dead tired. Do you know how that feels? One day I felt like I was at the end, and I started to resent all the travel, the letters, and many other things. One morning when I was lying in bed I talked it over with the Lord. The Lord showed me, through the Holy Spirit, that I had the sin of resentment. I had started to argue when I remembered that Jesus cannot cleanse an excuse, so I confessed my sin and told the Lord that I was willing to do whatever He had for me.

My joy became so full when I read in *The Living Bible*, Ephesians 3.14–19:

When I think of the wisdom . . . and scope of his plan I fall down on my knees and pray to the Father

73

of all the great family of God – some of them already in heaven and some down here on earth – that out of his glorious, unlimited resources he will give you the mighty inner strengthening of his Holy Spirit. And I pray that Christ will be more and more at home in your hearts, living within you as you trust in him. May your roots go down deep into the soil of God's marvellous love; and may you be able to feel and understand, as all God's children should, how long, how wide, how deep, and how high his love really is; and to experience this love for yourselves, though it is so great that you will never see the end of it or fully know or understand it. And so at last you will be filled up with God himself.

That encouraged me to know and trust that the unlimited resources of His strength are more than sufficient. I started to praise and thank the Lord, and my tiredness disappeared.

'Surely I have composed and quieted my soul; / Like a weaned child rests against his mother / My soul is like a weaned child within me' (Psalm 131.2 NASB).

Worry is like a rocking chair; it keeps you busy but does not bring you farther.

Learning to Forgive*

> ' For if ye forgive men their trespasses, your heavenly
> Father will also forgive you: But if ye forgive not
> men their trespasses, neither will your Father forgive
> your trespasses.'
>
> Matthew 6.14,15 KJV

It was in a church in Munich that I saw him, a balding
heavy-set man in a grey overcoat, a brown felt hat
clutched between his hands. People were filing out of
the basement room where I had just spoken, moving
along the rows of wooden chairs to the door at the
rear. It was 1947 and I had come from Holland to
defeated Germany with the message that God forgives.

It was the truth they needed most to hear in that
bitter, bombed-out land, and I gave them my favourite
mental picture. Maybe because the sea is never far
from a Hollander's mind, I liked to think that that's
where forgiven sins were thrown. 'When we confess
our sins,' I said, 'God casts them into the deepest
ocean, gone forever.'

The solemn faces stared back at me, not quite
daring to believe. There were never questions after a
talk in Germany in 1947. People stood up in silence,

in silence collected their wraps, in silence left the room.

And that's when I saw him, working his way forward against the others. One moment I saw the overcoat and the brown hat; the next, a blue uniform and a vizored cap with its skull and crossbones. It came back with a rush: the huge room with its harsh overhead lights, the pathetic pile of dresses and shoes in the centre of the floor, the shame of walking naked past this man. I could see my sister's frail form ahead of me, ribs sharp beneath the parchment skin. Betsie, how thin you were!

Betsie and I had been arrested for concealing Jews in our home during the Nazi occupation of Holland; this man had been a guard at Ravensbrück concentration camp where we were sent.

Now he was in front of me, hand thrust out: 'A fine message, *Fräulein!* How good it is to know that, as you say, all our sins are at the bottom of the sea!'

And I, who had spoken so glibly of forgiveness, fumbled in my wallet rather than take that hand. He would not remember me, of course – how could he remember one prisoner among those thousands of women?

But I remembered him and the leather crop swinging from his belt. It was the first time since my release that I had been face to face with one of my captors and my blood seemed to freeze.

'You mentioned Ravensbrück in your talk,' he was saying. 'I was a guard in there.' No, he did not remember me.

'But since that time,' he went on, 'I have become a Christian. I know that God has forgiven me for the cruel things I did there, but I would like to hear it

76

from your lips as well. *Fräulein*—' again the hand came out – 'will you forgive me?'

And I stood there – I whose sins had every day to be forgiven – and could not. Betsie had died in that place – could he erase her slow terrible death simply for the asking?

It could not have been many seconds that he stood there, hand held out, but to me it seemed hours as I wrestled with the most difficult thing I had ever had to do.

For I had to do it – I knew that. The message that God forgives has a prior condition: that we forgive those who have injured us. 'If you do not forgive men their trespasses,' Jesus says, 'neither will your Father in heaven forgive your trespasses.'

I knew it not only as a commandment of God, but as a daily experience. Since the end of the war I had had a home in Holland for victims of Nazi brutality. Those who were able to forgive their former enemies were able also to return to the outside world and rebuild their lives, no matter what the physical scars. Those who nursed bitterness remained invalids. It was as simple and as horrible as that.

And still I stood there with the coldness clutching my heart. But forgiveness is not an emotion – I knew that too. Forgiveness is an act of the will, and the will can function regardless of the temperature of the heart. 'Jesus, help me!' I prayed silently. 'I can lift my hand. I can do that much. You supply the feeling.'

And so woodenly, mechanically, I thrust my hand into the one stretched out to me. And as I did, an incredible thing took place. The current started in my shoulder, raced down my arm, sprang into our joined hands. And then this healing warmth seemed to flood my whole being, bringing tears to my eyes.

77

'I forgive you, brother!' I cried. 'With all my heart!'

For a long moment we grasped each other's hands, the former guard and the former prisoner. I had never known God's love so intensely as I did then.

God gives forgiveness for what we have done, but we also need deliverance from who we are.

Jesus did not say, 'Thou shalt not be tempted and thou shalt not be afflicted.' But He did say, 'Thou shalt not be overcome!'

The battle is not ours, but God's.

God never inspires doubt and fear but rather faith and courage.

'For because he himself has suffered and been tempted, he is able to help those who are tempted' (Hebrews 2.18 RSV).

Bearing One Another's Burdens

> *'And the Lord restored the fortunes of Job when he prayed for his friends . . .'*
>
> Job 42.10 NASB

What a joy it is to know that the Holy Spirit leads us when we have an opportunity to counsel people. When we need help, we can cash the cheque given in James 1.5: 'If any of you lacks wisdom, let him ask God, who gives to all men generously and without reproaching, and it will be given him' (RSV).

I once had a talk with a student who suffered from nervous tension. Although the Lord performed a miracle of liberation, the boy still seemed rather absentminded. Then the Lord guided my approach to him.

'Will you do something for me?' I asked. 'I have a problem. My prayer time is so attacked by the enemy. As soon as I start to pray, all kinds of thoughts start to distract me.

'There was a time in my life when unclean thoughts came into my heart the moment I would concentrate on praying. But this is past. Now they are clean, practical questions, such as, "At what time must I speak tomorrow? Who is taking care of transportation? Are there enough vegetables and potatoes for Sunday?" All very good thoughts, but they hinder my concentration for prayer. Will you pray with me that the Lord will make me free and protect my prayer time?'

He did, and his prayer was something unusual – so dedicated, so understanding, so full of love. He showed a real burden for my problem!

'I am sure you have a ministry of intercession,' I told him.

'I believe it, too,' he answered.

At that moment I saw that his absent-mindedness was gone. He was free. He became a real prayer partner from that day on. The moment he started to do something for another, he was free from self, with all its complications. And my prayer life was healed.

Another ministry of the Holy Spirit, I have discovered, is revealing our sins to us. While travelling around the world and meeting so many Christians, I found two attitudes toward sin. One is the easy way: 'I am just human. Nobody is perfect.' The other puts people under a permanent burden about past and present sins, not realizing the finished work of Jesus Christ on the cross.

In the power of the Lord Jesus Christ we stand on victory ground. He has lifted us out of the old vicious circle of sin and death (see Romans 8.2). From the circle of sinning, fighting, and conquering but always sinning again, fighting, failing, and so on, Jesus has brought us inside His blessed circle of repentance, forgiveness, and cleansing by His blood (see 1 John 1.7,9).

The devil is not yet on pension! He is very active, but he is no longer victorious in the 'blessed circle' where Jesus Christ has placed us. Whom Jesus makes free is free indeed, but to live this victorious life you must not leave the confessing of your sins until later. The door of repentance is wide open. Hallelujah!

Commitment

God never gives power to be a martyr in advance.

When we deepen our message, then God will expand our ministry.

In witnessing, our primary function is proclamation, not defence.

Brilliance is sterile unless it is coupled with commitment.

A visitor saw a nurse attending the sores of a leprosy patient. 'I would not do that for a million dollars,' she said. The nurse answered, 'Neither would I, but I do it for Jesus for nothing.'

Going to church doesn't make you a Christian any more than going to a garage makes you a car.

No Fishing Allowed*

> 'My little children, I am telling you this so that you
> will stay away from sin. But if you sin, there is
> someone to plead for you before the Father. His name
> is Jesus . . .'
>
> 1 John 2.1 TLB

'Hallelujah!' Handel's chorus resounded through the
evening air. 'Hallelujah! And He shall reign for ever
and ever.'

I had never heard it sung so perfectly and in such
beautiful surroundings.

We were in Japan. The moon and stars were clear,
in a special way as they can only be in that country.
Far away we even saw the white peak of Mount Fuji.

'Hallelujah! The Lord God omnipotent reigneth.'

I had never heard it sung *a capella*, without musical
accompaniment. It was as if angels were singing.

I knew the girls [in the choir]. They were the
students for whom I had been holding a daily Bible
study for the last two weeks, and they were going to
the same hall as I, where I was expected to answer
questions.

That evening I listened most to their worry about
sins. I prayed that the Lord would give me clear

*From *He is More than Able*, pp. 83–85, copyright © 1978 by Corrie
ten Boom. Used by permission of Kingsway Publications.

answers for them. They were Christian girls, but what a lack of joy they had about the finished work of Jesus at the cross. I asked them a question. 'When you rehearsed the "Hallelujah Chorus," did you make mistakes?'

The girls giggled. Japanese girls giggle much.

'Many.'

'But when you were singing outside in that Japanese moonlit evening, you did not think of those mistakes, otherwise you might have repeated them. Girls, never wait to confess your sins. The devil accuses us night and day. I will tell you something. Sunday morning I spoke in your church.'

'Yes, we remember it. You gave us much, but it was so short.'

'I thought the same and your pastor had promised me a long time [to speak]. I asked him, "Because I can speak only once in your church, give me as long as possible. Make your preliminaries short." He promised me but did not do it. We started the service at ten o'clock and at eleven o'clock he was still busy with the *Book of Common Prayer*. That moment the Holy Spirit showed me that I was very impatient. I knew that [impatience is] a sin, and at eleven o'clock I brought it to the Lord and asked forgiveness. When we confess our sins, He is faithful and just to forgive us and to cleanse us with His blood. Suddenly I saw that the words of the *Book of Common Prayer* were not just preliminaries, but truths that the Lord uses for His honour.

'Why did I tell you that it was eleven o'clock? Because the devil accuses us before God and our own hearts. It is possible that he said to God at 11:05, "Do You see Corrie ten Boom in Your church and how impatient she is?" I believe that God answered him,

"I already know it. Five minutes ago Corrie told me. It is forgiven and cleansed."

'Girls, be sure that you are always five minutes earlier than the accuser. Then you lose your worry about your sins. The reason Jesus came to earth was to save sinners. He died for you, so you could be forgiven, and He lives for you and in you by His Holy Spirit, to make you overcomers. When you worry about your sins it is because you know them through the accuser who has told you, "That sin is typically yours. That is your nature; you will remain like that your whole life. There is no hope for you."

'The devil, the accuser, is a liar. When the Holy Spirit convicts you of sin it is always in the floodlight of the finished work of Jesus at the cross. He tells you: "Exactly for these sins Jesus died. Confess and be cleansed."

'Do you remember what I taught you this week – what the Bible says about repented sins? "As far as the east is from the west, so far hath he removed our transgressions from us" [Psalm 103.12 KJV]. He throws them into the depths of the sea, forgiven and forgotten, and to warn the accuser He puts a sign saying No Fishing Allowed. Girls, instead of worrying about your sins, sing again, "Hallelujah! King of kings and Lord of lords." '

It sounded even more beautiful than when I had heard it outside. But this time I saw happy faces, some wet with tears.

Awakening to God's Peace

In Corrie's thirty-three years of travelling, she experienced many once-in-a-lifetime events. While travelling in India, she had the opportunity to take a trip on an elephant, and upon her return she wrote her impressions of that journey.

I used to have the idea that a jungle meant wild life full of thrills and surprises – a wild west experience. It is quite different. Of course, in jungle life wild beasts do kill each other and the struggle for life is constant and brutal, but I saw another side of the picture.

We arose very early in the morning after sleeping in a forest bungalow on top of a hill in the jungle. It was five o'clock when we started our trip. Our party was divided on the backs of two elephants.

It was dark in the jungle and we were quiet, for we hoped to see wild animals. If they hear voices they keep their distance, so the only noise was the breaking of branches under the feet of our elephants.

It was like a dream. Far in the east there seemed to come a light; the breath and whisper of dawn brought a promise of the coming day. The birds started singing and whistling – different from any whistling I had ever heard before. The jungle was awakening.

Slowly, very slowly, we moved through the wild woods. Sometimes the man in front of us would cut away the branches that could hurt us. It was all so peaceful, so quiet and restful.

This was enjoying nature – no hurry, for time does not count. Deer passed us at a short distance. They were not afraid of us, because we had become a part of the jungle for them. It became lighter and we could see the monkeys high up in the trees jumping from one treetop to another, odd fellows, full of mischief.

The sky in the east coloured beautifully, and it was chilly. It reminded me of the coldness we felt at roll-call in the concentration camp. I learned then that the coldest time of the day is about twenty minutes before sunrise, when the temperature drops.

I thought of the great change in my life. Then I was a prisoner. Now I was free, so free that I could go around the world, even through a jungle in India. I felt so happy with my blessed life. There was a kind of heavenly joy in my heart, for I thought of the time when the sun of righteousness shall shine upon the earth and 'the earth shall be full of the knowledge of the LORD as the waters cover the sea' (Isaiah 11.9 KJV). I experienced a foretaste of the time when there will be peace on earth as there now is in heaven.

Suddenly, as the sunbeams shot through the trees, it was as if life increased in the jungle, and we began to see more animals. Two men who were walking noiselessly before us gave us a sign to stop. They looked at the footprints on the ground and whispered, 'Bison.' The elephants stood motionless. Then we saw them, a herd of twenty, thirty, perhaps even forty bison! They also saw us, and gazing curiously in our direction, they too stood motionless.

What did they intend to do? I told myself that if

they should come and surround us, the elephants would become unruly and throw us down. But I could not think of panic. This was all so natural and peaceful; and even if something were to happen, why fear? The best is yet to be!

The bison turned and moved away. Carefully the elephants stepped down into a little steep valley. It is wonderful how these enormous animals can walk so securely on a small path, even up and down, feeling their way with the tips of their trunks.

How well I would remember this jungle. When I was in the midst of the noise of the big cities, when I had to find my way through the jungle of Times Square in New York City or the Ginza Nishu in Tokyo, it helped me to know that there are jungles where there is an abundance of time, quietness, and beautiful nature and where it is possible to travel only six miles in four hours, as we did. Here our eyes grasped more and enjoyed beauty that would never be seen during the thousands of miles travelled at high speeds in aeroplanes and cars.

The elephants knelt down. It was the end of our trip. Some black hands kindly helped me to the ground, and I felt as refreshed as if I had had two weeks' holiday.

Our Hands in His

*'But thanks be to God, who in Christ always leads us
in triumph, and through us spreads the fragrance of
the knowledge of him everywhere.'*

2 Corinthians 2.14 RSV

Sometimes the responsibility of all my work has
burdened me. There is so much to do, and we all
understand that we must redeem the time, because
the days are evil (see Ephesians 5.16). What joy that
we may and must surrender everything.

When I talked my concern over with the Lord, He
showed me an empty suitcase. He said: 'You possess
nothing, you have surrendered all, so you have no
responsibilities at all. I carry all responsibilities, you
are only my steward.'

What joy came into my heart! I prayed; 'O Lord, let
me see You a moment.' 'Look at your left hand,' He
said. I saw that my hand was in another hand. That
hand was pierced . . . it was Jesus' hand. I never
before understood what surrender meant – our weak
hand in Jesus' strong hand! His strength in our life!
Surrender to the Lord Jesus is dynamic and relaxed.
What joy! Hallelujah!

Look to Jesus*

> 'God is able to make all grace abound toward you;
> that ye, always having all sufficiency in all things,
> may abound to every good work.'
>
> 2 Corinthians 9.8 KJV

In Germany I once spoke to young people about the riches we possess in Christ Jesus. Germans are reticent, and when I asked them to stay for an after-talk, only seven remained. Soon we broke the ice.

One said, 'I am an atheist. You do it with Jesus, I do it without Him and just as well.' When he told of what he had achieved in his own strength, I did not say much. I am not much good at arguing. Silently I prayed for him while listening, and then I said: 'Should there ever come a time in your life when you cannot work in your own strength, then think of what you heard tonight.'

Then another young man began to talk, and he said, 'Once I was a soldier of Hitler; now I am a soldier of Jesus. To me the Bible is an accounting of all I possess in Him. I followed Hitler wholeheartedly; God struck everything out of my hands. I was in prison, and in that prison camp a comrade read the Bible with me every day. Then I saw.'

After that, the others told of their difficulties. One

*This story is also told in *Amazing Love* by Corrie ten Boom, pp. 46–47. Copyright © 1953 by Christian Literature Crusade, London.

girl said, 'I am so unfaithful. I am willing, but my faith is so unequal. Now that you have told me so much, I feel certain, but tomorrow? I don't know whether I shall succeed then.'

'When I was a watchmaker, sometimes I had new watches that did not run well,' I told her. 'I did not repair them myself, but returned them to the manufacturer. When he had repaired them, they ran perfectly. This is what I do with my faith. Jesus is the Author and Finisher of our faith. If it does not work well, I return it to the heavenly Manufacturer. And when He has repaired it, it works perfectly!'

Let us look more and more at Jesus, not at our faith. Let us not consider the gales around us, but Him; then we can walk on the waves. Faith is such a firm ground that the safest path to walk on is the sea on which Peter walked towards Jesus.

Of itself, our conversation changed into a prayer meeting. The 'atheist' also folded his hands and closed his eyes.

We will not be rewarded for what we achieved but rather for our faithfulness.

When God is second, you will get the second best, but when God is really first, you have His best.

From the Old Chest

'The path of the righteous is the light of dawn,
That shines brighter and brighter until the full day'
Proverbs 4.18 NASB

My nephew, Peter van Woerden, and I wrote a book dealing with our ancestry, and much of the material was taken from letters and documents found in an old chest. There were many interesting items in that chest!

Here is a letter I wrote in 1916 to some of my friends.*

January 30, 1916

Dear Girls,

Last night I had an interesting dream. Before I forget it, I want to tell you all about it. It was so exciting. The funny thing was that all during my dream I was conscious that these things were happening many, many years before I was born. It was the time when my great-grandfather Gerrit was gardener in the Bronstede Estate. Father has often told me about this man's faith, courage, and patriotism. Now here is my dream.

I was walking over a rough street with cobblestones and thought I had never had such an interesting adven-

*The letter was first published, in part, in Father ten Boom: God's Man, copyright © 1978 by Corrie ten Boom, pp. 116–117, and the paragraph following the letter is from p. 22 of the same publication. Used by permission of Kingsway Publications.

ture. The people I saw had different clothing from what I had on. Old-fashioned carriages passed me – a long train of gigs with many horses in front. I realized that I walked there in the time when the princes of Orange still reigned in our country.

I saw an old inn at the side of the road. I went in and saw an interior like a Frans Hals painting: men sitting there with broadbrimmed hats on, smoking long pipes and sitting on rough chairs beside windows with small window panes. But the birds outside were singing just as in our time. The trees and flowers were not different from ours.

I did not say anything, but the people seemed to know who I was and the innkeeper said, 'That man over there is Master ten Boom. I am sure you are interested in meeting him.'

My forefather greeted me kindly but did not seem amazed to see someone who would live a hundred years later. 'Come with me,' he said, 'My wife will be glad to meet you.'

On the way to his home we did not talk much, but when I saw the old-fashioned carriages I said, 'Perhaps I could visit the prince of Orange; he certainly would like to meet someone who will live many years after today.'

'That would take much, much time,' Great-grandfather said. 'The prince lives in the Hague. How are you going to get there?' I suddenly realized that there were not yet any trains or cars. It would take me days to get there.

Very quickly we were in the kitchen where Great-grandmother was cooking a meal. They sat down at the table to eat, and I sat next to the window. A boy of about ten took off his cap and they all prayed silently. 'Is that boy my grandfather?' I thought to myself. After the meal, Great-grandfather took his Bible and read a portion.

'Child,' he said, 'when your time to live comes, much

will be different from what you see here around you. But this Book will be the same. If anyone undertakes to change it, then know that it is wrong. The Word of God is the same for ever and ever.'

He took my hand and led me to the garden. I saw how he put some seed into the earth. 'This seed will give flowers. Before they die they will give seed. And so it will go on. In your days, there will still be flowers that come forth from this seed. In the same way it will go with the ten Booms. You will exist many years after I shall have died.'

This was the end of my dream, but I was strangely moved. I like what I have dreamed about the Bible. 'Heaven and earth will pass away, but God's Word will never pass away.' I only doubt if I will ever enjoy a new translation.

> God bless you girls,
> Your Corrie

We are surrounded by a cloud of witnesses.

Great-grandfather Gerrit's life was one of those seeds that was to bear fruit later. In one of the letters his house was referred to as 'a house of prayer.' Some thirty years after his death, the church in Heemstede became the scene of a fresh revival under the ministry of a godly pastor, Nicolaas Beets. Gerrit's prayers and tears had not been in vain. The lessons of history teach us patience. As a Dutch saying has it, 'God's mills often grind slowly, but they grind surely.'

Is Baptism Important?

> '*Whatever happens, make sure that your everyday life is worthy of the gospel of Christ.*'
>
> Philippians 1.27 PHILLIPS

In Germany I once spoke to a men's club of Lutherans and Baptists. There was great blessing, and I felt that together we were listening to the Holy Spirit, who was teaching us.

After I had spoken there were a few testimonies, and the Lord was praised for His great deeds. Then the question came: 'What do you think is the scriptural way of baptizing?'

This question I felt to be a wile of the devil. The blessing would vanish if the rest of the time were used for discussion about baptism. I prayed for wisdom. I am so thankful for James 1.5: 'If any of you lack wisdom, let him ask of God, that giveth to all men liberally, and upbraideth not; and it shall be given him' (KJV).

I replied; 'Let us read the last words the Lord Jesus spoke on earth in Mark 16.15–18. "And he said unto them, Go ye into all the world and preach the gospel to every creature. He that believeth and is baptized shall be saved; but he that believeth not shall be damned. And these signs shall follow them that believe; In my name shall they cast out devils; they shall speak with new tongues; They shall take up serpents; and if they drink any deadly thing, it shall not hurt them; they shall lay hands on the sick, and they shall recover" [KJV].

'Here we find three important commandments Jesus gave: 1. World evangelization. 2. Baptism. 3. The gifts of the Spirit.

'What about the first of these? Do you do all you can to bring the gospel to the whole world by preaching, praying, and giving?

'What about the third? Are captives being released because of your obedience, in His strength, to the Lord's commandment? Are sick people being healed in Jesus' name?

'If with regard to the first and the third there is something lacking in your life, there is still much work for you to do. As soon as you have finished this, come to me again and I shall tell you what I think of the second matter.

'But I can tell you now that it certainly is not God's intention to make a controversy of baptism. We must obey His commands, though, and we may enjoy baptism as a great, joyful privilege.'

God gave me the wisdom I needed. We had a wonderful evening together and continued to witness.

Should Women Preach?

Corrie was interviewed once on the subject of women who preach. The following is a portion of that interview.

Question: Have you ever had the difficulty that some people do not like women to speak in public?

Answer: No, because I have never been where they do not allow me to go.

Question: But do you not have the feeling that you are being disobedient? Paul says in 1 Timothy 2.11,12 and 1 Corinthians 14.34,35 that women must be silent.

Answer: Yes, that is so, but we must know what these words mean and what they do not mean. We must find their meaning for the present age. Peter gave us a sketch of the present age in the words of Joel, 'I will pour forth my Spirit upon all flesh; and your sons and daughters shall prophesy . . .' (Acts 2.17 KJV). Now, what is prophecy? First Corinthians 14.3 says, 'edification, exhortation, and comfort.'

Question: But did Peter not mean that these things happened at the first Pentecost (see Acts 2.16–21)?

Answer: Yes, they partly happened then, but in carrying on with the quotation he talked of things which were not then happening. 'Blood, and fire, and vapour of smoke' (Acts 2.19) have not yet come to pass, nor the sun being 'turned into darkness' and the 'moon into blood' (Acts 2.20). We know from other Scriptures that this will happen before the return of the Lord Jesus (see Matthew 24.29; Revelation 6.12). We live in days past the beginning of the prophecy and before the end of it. Acts 2.18 quotes Joel, 'Upon my male and female slaves [the literal meaning] will I pour forth of my Spirit and they shall prophesy.' There is no distinction of race in this verse; the power is to any devoted servant of Christ, Jew or Gentile, male or female. The one hundred and twenty on the first Pentecost included certain women, and they were all filled with the Holy Spirit and all spoke languages they had never learned (see Acts 1.13–15; 2.1–11).

In 1 Corinthians 11.5 we find that women prophesied in the assembly, and this was not forbidden by Paul but merely regulated – the covering of the head being commanded. This verse also tells that women prayed in the church. In Acts 21.9 it is told that Philip's four daughters prophesied, not because it was rare for women to prophesy, but that it was unusual for four women in one family to do so.

Question: But what about 1 Corinthians 14.34 and 35, where it is clearly said that women must keep silent in the churches?

Answer: I believe that this must be interpreted in the light of these other Scriptures and not in conflict with them. Here is meant silence while another is speaking. ('Let them ask their own husbands at home' – 1 Corinthians 14.35). I believe that Miriam, Deborah, and Anna (who were prophetesses) are good company for me. And Psalm 68.11, in the original, gives them and me the encouragement, 'The women who proclaim the good tidings are a great host . . .' (NASB). There is one thing that neither man nor woman can be without – the anointing of the Holy Spirit which equips us to speak for God (see Acts 2.18).

We are ambassadors for Christ. What is an ambassador? He is sent forth in an official capacity by a nation's government to represent that government in the territory of another nation. His authority is not measured by his own personal ability but is in direct proportion to the authority of the government he represents.

Freedom is not the right to do what we want but the power to do what we ought.

God's Special People

Before World War II began, Corrie was involved in working to bring the gospel to mentally handicapped people. She later wrote a booklet about these experiences entitled Common Sense Not Needed. *The following stories are excerpts from that booklet.**

Bringing the gospel to mentally handicapped people is not important work in the eyes of the world. To convert a 'big shot' is more important than to save a mentally handicapped person who cannot organize a mission, cannot start a drive to collect money, cannot write books, and cannot do what splendid, gifted Christians can.

Does heaven have the same standards as earth? I do not think so.

I believe that the joy of the angels of God when a handicapped person is converted is as great as when a 'big shot' gives his heart and life to Jesus. It is possible that the joy is greater; heaven is different from earth. One can never tell.

I had spoken to our boys about prayer. Jake, the tramp, accompanied me home. (My friends often said, 'Such dignified friends you walk around with!')

*From *Common Sense Not Needed*, copyright © 1957 by Corrie ten Boom, pp. 25–26,28. Used by permission of Christian Literature Crusade, London.

First he told me how he had set up in business. He had taken the door off his room and chopped it up into small pieces to make firewood. He had sold the wood, going from door to door. This was good business in Holland during the war. Cost: not one cent. Profit: enough money for many weeks. It was not easy to persuade Jake that what he did was stealing.

'Jake, do you know what prayer is?' I asked.

At first he was silent.

'Do you mean like this?' Jake asked hesitatingly. 'Often I feel something I can't push away.'

'That's it, Jake! Praying is asking Jesus to push away what you cannot push yourself. Jesus can do everything and He loves you so much that He wants to push away the bad things in your life.'

Next day I had something I could not 'push away.' I was down-hearted and the spirit of worry was in my heart. Then I remembered the conversation with Jake and I asked, 'Lord Jesus, will you push away the worry?'

And He did.

Anton was a Mongoloid. He could neither speak nor walk alone. He was in my class for a very short time. He listened to my Bible stories, but when I spoke too long to suit him, he yawned . . . I did not know how much Anton really understood.

Once I took his hand and touched his five fingers one after another and said, 'Jesus loves Anton so much.' The next week, when Anton saw me, he took my hand and with his fingers outspread, looked at me with a face full of longing. 'Jesus loves Anton so much,' I repeated, touching a finger at every word. Then I taught him to do it himself.

After that, every week, Anton showed me with his fingers how much Jesus loved him. The last time I saw him, I told him while he touched his left fingers with his right hand, 'Jesus loves Anton so much. How thankful I am for that! You too, Anton?'

'Yes,' Anton said, as his face lit up.

It was the only word I ever heard from Anton. It is the most worthwhile word that any person can speak to the Lord Jesus.

Where there is faith, there is love
Where there is love, there is peace
Where there is peace, there is blessing
Where there is blessing, there is God
Where there is God, there is no want.

A religion that is small enough for our understanding would not be big enough for our needs.

Choices

'He will keep you steadfast in the faith to the end, so that when his day comes you need fear no condemnation.'

1 Corinthians 1.8 PHILLIPS

Several years ago I was in Vietnam. It was one of the times I suffered with the people in the war. I remember that I went as far as I could go through the jungle and rice paddies to the front lines so I could speak to the American G.I.'s – young men, yes, in my eyes still boys. Their life was hard. Days and days they had to live in the jungle. They suffered and made people suffer.

We heard around us bombs falling and the 'ric-a-tic' of machine guns. The soldiers were thankful – almost too happy – for a visit from an old lady who had come from a country where there was peace. And now I was with them on the battlefield. They seldom saw women there, perhaps only the prostitutes. I had such pity for them.

I tried first to tell them all the jokes I could remember in English. Then I said, 'Now boys, I want to talk "turkey".' (I tried to use some slang I had learned from the students.) 'There are two possibilities. Either you come through the war alive or you fall in action. Let us think a moment if that last thing happens. Are you ready to meet a righteous God?

Are you not ready? Come to Jesus. He is willing and able to prepare you.'

A lady told me later that her son had written her from Vietnam: 'Now I know what it means to receive Jesus Christ as my Saviour. I did it and what peace there is in my heart.' Three weeks later he fell in action.

Just as you received Christ, so go on living in Him, in simple faith (see Colossians 2.6).

Faith is not just 'believing'; faith is relating yourself to a person. If I commit myself to a chair, it is not the strength of my commitment that holds me up, but the strength of the chair.

Trust

A man who gives all to God will lose nothing.

Jesus, confirm my heart's desire
To work and speak and think for Thee;
Still let me guard the holy fires,
And still stir up Thy gift in me.

It is a wonderful life that is guided by a God who never makes mistakes. The only condition laid upon us is obedience.

Faith brings us on highways that make our reasoning dizzy.

To have what we want is riches, but to be able to do without is power.

Let God's promises shine on your problems.

A Christmas Wish

*'I came that they might have life, and might have it
abundantly.'*

John 10.10 NASB

What do I wish for you for Christmas? That you may
have the joy the shepherds had (see Luke 2.15–20).

The shepherds told everyone what had happened.
They knew so much more than the other people in
Bethlehem. They had heard the angel's message
which the Lord had made known to them; they had
seen the newborn babe. They had met Mary and
Joseph. What did they do? They told everyone! Do
we know more than those for whom Christmas means
only 'Jingle Bells' and Santa Claus or who only
prepare for Christmas by getting cards off at the right
time and presents wrapped? They are trying to do
their yearly duty, for they have done this ritual every
year, afraid of what others will think if they don't.

Christmas is not a duty! Jesus' coming was a free
gift to all of us. The only thing we can do is to prepare
ourselves for His coming.

Christmas is a remembrance of His coming as a
little baby. Let us be ready for that feast so that we
can prepare others too.

What a joy to know Him, Jesus Christ, who was
born in Bethlehem, died at the cross for our sins, was

resurrected, and is with us always unto the end of the world.

Let us do what the shepherds did, and tell everyone who will listen.

'His unchanging plan has always been to adopt us into His own family by sending Jesus Christ to die for us. And He did this because He wanted to! Now all praise to God for His wonderful kindness to us and His favour that He has poured out upon us, because we belong to His dearly loved Son' (Ephesians 1.5,6 TLB).

When Will Jesus Come?

'Whatever we may have to go through now is less than nothing compared with the magnificent future God has in store for us.'

Romans 8.18 PHILLIPS

Can we expect that Jesus will return soon? I think we can, and I am looking forward to it, full of expectation. What a joy when He will do that which He promises in Revelation 21.5: 'I make all things new.'

Will God's children have to pass through the great tribulation? Many expect that we shall be taken away before it comes. But now already there is a terrible battle going on between the powers of the kingdom of light and those of the kingdom of darkness. Is not every Christian more or less on the front line? But we know that those who are with us are much stronger and more numerous than those who are against us.

What joy to know that Jesus said: 'In the world ye shall have tribulation: but be of good cheer; I have overcome the world' (John 16.33 KJV). And when the situation grows worse and worse and our hearts nearly faint for fear, will not then the time have come to 'look up, and lift up your heads; for your redemption draweth nigh' (Luke 21.28 KJV)?

The world needs strong and trusting Christians, especially during the time of tribulation. It needs Christians who see the reality of God's plan and of

Jesus' victory. 'Where there is no vision, the people perish . . .' (Proverbs 29.18 KJV).

For each one personally it will be very important whether the Lord Jesus is our Judge or our Saviour. Do not wait to accept Him; do it now. One day it will be too late.

I do not know when Jesus will come again. I do not know the hour or the day, but I know that He will come and that there is no hour or day when He could not come.

'And now, . . . abide in him; that, when he shall appear, we may have confidence, and not be ashamed before him at his coming' (1 John 2.28 KJV).

'May the God of peace himself sanctify you wholly; and may your spirit and soul and body be kept sound and blameless at the coming of our Lord Jesus Christ' (1 Thessalonians 5.23 ʀsv).

Acknowledgements

Scripture quotations from the King James Version of the Bible (marked KJV) are Crown Copyright, and are used by permission.

Scripture quotations from the Revised Standard Version of the Bible (marked RSV), copyrighted 1946, 1952, © 1971, 1973 by the Division of Christian Education of the National Council of the Churches of Christ in the USA, are used by permission.

Scripture quotations from the New American Standard Bible (marked NASB), © The Lockman Foundation 1960, 1962, 1963, 1968, 1971, 1972, 1973, 1975, are used by permission.

Scripture quotations from The Living Bible (marked TLB), © Tyndale House Publishers, USA 1971, are used by permission.

Scripture quotations from J. B. Phillips: The New Testament in Modern English (rev. ed.) (marked PHILLIPS) are used by permission of Macmillan Publishers Ltd.